element

volume 6 issue 2
fall 2015

the journal of
the society for
mormon philosophy
and theology

Copyright © 2016 The Society for Mormon Philosophy and Theology
Published in the USA by Greg Kofford Books
ISSN: 1947-9719
Volume 6, Issue 2 ISBN: 978-1-58958-511-9

Greg Kofford Books
P.O. Box 1362
Draper, UT 84020
www.gregkofford.com

element

the journal of the society for mormon philosophy and theology

EDITORS:

Carrie A. and James M. Mclachlan,
Western Carolina University

ASSOCIATE EDITORS:

Loyd Isao Ericson
Mark Olsen
Dan Wotherspoon

SOCIETY FOR MORMON PHILOSOPHY AND THEOLOGY

Element is the official publication of the Society for Mormon Philosophy and Theology. The Society brings together scholars and others who share an interest in studying the teachings and texts of the Church of Jesus Christ of Latter-day Saints. It facilitates the sharing and discussion of work by sponsoring an annual conference, and publishing this journal. Its statement of purpose reads as follows:

> *The purpose of the Society is to promote disciplined reflection on Latter-day Saint beliefs. Its aims include constructive engagement with the broader tradition of philosophy and theology. All its publications, conferences, and other forums for discussion will take seriously both the commitments of faith and the standards of scholarship.*

SUBMISSION AND REPRINT INFORMATION

Submissions should be sent as attachments via e-mail to James M. McLachlan, editor, at JMCLACHLA@EMAIL.WCU.EDU in Microsoft Word format. An abstract of no more than 150 words should accompany each submission along with full contact information, including name, title, institution, phone numbers, e-mail, and mailing addresses. All articles will be subject to blind review and editorial modification.

Contents

The Mormon Jesus
and the Nicene Christ

by Richard J. Mouw

O ver the recent years I have received several scoldings from evangelicals for being too easy on Mormonism. One instance that raised considerable fire focused particularly on Christology. In an afterword that I wrote to Robert Millet's book *A Different Jesus? The Christ of the Latter-day Saints* I said that in spite of the many objections that I have to the Mormon perspective on Christ that Millet sets forth, I am convinced nonetheless "that Bob Millet is in fact trusting in the Jesus of the Bible for his salvation."[1]

I am not going to defend here my positive evaluation of the state of Robert Millet's soul, except to say that there is an important distinction to be made between judging that a person loves the Jesus of the New Testament and judging that the same person's Christological formulation falls within the boundaries of theological orthodoxy as defined by the classical Christian tradition. Whether a person has a proper relationship to the Christ of the Scriptures can be assessed—insofar as we humans can assess such things—by the evidence in that the person is relying on God's mercy to cultivate a life that manifests a Christ-like spirit. And we may give a person high marks in that regard while at the same time judging that the person offers highly defective theological formulations about the person and work of Jesus Christ. As Gerald McDermott put it recently in a *First Things* exchange with Bruce Porter, in insisting that Mormon theology is a regrettable departure from

---

1. Richard J. Mouw, afterword to Robert L. Millet, *A Different Jesus? The Christ of the Latter-day Saints* (Grand Rapids: William B. Eerdmans Publishing Co., 2005), 183.

Christian teaching, he is not "talking about whether Mormons can be saved, which is a different matter."[2]

To say that the Mormon theological system falls outside of the boundaries of normative Christian teaching is simply to take seriously the statements of LDS authorities themselves. Chief among these statements, of course, is the oft-quoted testimony of Joseph Smith in his account of his First Vision, that when he inquired of the divine Personage "which of all the sects was right," he was told "that all their creeds were an abomination in his sight."[3]

To be sure, recent LDS scholars have done some impressive work in putting this stark condemnation of Christian creeds in context. A case in point is John Welch's insightful essay on the history of creedalism, where he argues that not all Christian creeds ought to be viewed by Mormons as being of equal negative value. Mormons should have little problem with the Apostles Creed, for example. The problem, says Welch, is that as things developed historically "the tendencies of creedal formulations went too far in the direction of definitive absolutism, taking away the liberty of the pure and simple spirit that had prevailed in the apostolic era," thereby "prescribing and imposing extensive definitions and boundaries on the faithful."[4]

That the Nicene Creed in particular looms large in this regard in the minds of Mormon leaders was made clear by the late Gordon B. Hinckley's verdict that "[w]e do not accept the Nicene Creed, nor any other creed based on tradition and the conclusions of men."[5]

*****

In one sense, of course, Mormons should have no real problem endorsing the central thesis of Nicaea's Christological formulation—namely, that the

---

2. The original exchange between McDermott and Porter was "Is Mormonism Christian?" *First Things*, October 2008; the comments quoted here are from McDermott in "Correspondence," *First Things,* February 2009, 9.

3. Joseph Smith, *History of the Church of Jesus Christ of Latter-day Saints*, ed. B. H. Roberts, 7 vols. (Salt Lake City: The Church of Jesus Christ of Latter-day Saints, 1950), 1:18–19.

4. John W. Welch, "'All Their Creeds Were an Abomination': A Brief Look at the Creeds as Part of the Apostasy," in *Prelude to the Restoration: From Apostasy to the Restored Church* (Provo, Utah and Salt Lake City: BYU Religious Studies Center and Deseret Book, 2004), 228–49, available at https://rsc.byu.edu/archived/prelude-restoration-apostasy-restored-church/all-their-creeds-were-abomination-brief-look (accessed Oct. 29, 2015).

5. Gordon B. Hinckley, "What are People Asking about Us?" *Ensign* (November 1998), at https://www.lds.org/ensign/1998/11/what-are-people-asking-about-us (accessed Oct. 29, 2015).

Son is of *homoousia,* "of one being," with God the Father. If we take that claim in isolation from everything else in the creed, it actually comports quite nicely with Mormon Christology. After all, Mormons are famous for having taught that the members of the Godhead and human beings are "of the same species."[6] This means that not only are the Father and the Son "of the same substance" but they also share that metaphysical character with all human beings.

That is exactly where the problem comes up between Mormons and the rest of us. And it is a problem that cuts deep. Judaism and Christianity have been united in their insistence that the Creator and the creation—including God's human creatures—are divided by an unbridgeable "being" gap. God is the "Wholly Other"—the *totaliter aliter,* eternal and self-sufficient—who is in a realm of existence that is radically distinct from the creation that was brought into being out of nothing by God's sovereign decree. With this view of things, to confuse the Creator's being with anything in his creation is to commit the sin of idolatry. The Mormon "same species" contention, on the other hand, sees the differences between God and humankind not in terms of an unbridgeable gap of being but as best expressed in the language of "more" and "less"—quantitative rather than qualitative differences.

So, does that leave us at an impasse, beyond which no significant dialogue is possible about the person and work of Christ? I think not. I want to point to two potentially productive foci for pursuing the conversation: soteriology (i.e., the theology of salvation) and the historical development of doctrine. I will briefly explain here how the conversations in each of those areas might go.

*****

Mormonism is often portrayed as a self-deification program—and not without some legitimacy given the popularity of the Lorenzo Snow couplet, to say nothing of some of the formulations in Joseph's "King Follett Discourse." But the fact is that there are strong elements in much of Mormon thought that are closely aligned with traditional Christian soteriology, with its insistence on a human sinfulness that requires nothing less than the atoning power of the heaven-sent Savior for our salvation. Here, for example, is the late Glenn L. Pearson, a longtime faculty member at Brigham Young University, describing, in his widely used primer of Mormon teachings, the proper spirit for entering into God's presence:

> There has to be down payment of a broken heart and a contrite spirit. Who has a broken heart and contrite spirit? One who is stripped of pride

---

6. See, for example, "Discourse by Elder O.F. Whitney," *The Latter-day Saints' Millennial Star* 57, no. 3 (January 17, 1895): 34.

and selfishness. One who has come down in the depths of humility and prostrated himself before the Lord in mighty prayer and supplication. He has realized the awful guilt of his sins and has pled for the blood of Christ to be a covering to shield himself from the face of a just God.[7]

More recently, Elder Jeffrey Holland, of the Quorum of the Twelve, described Christ's redemptive mission in this way:

> [I]n a spiritual agony that began in Gethsemane and a physical payment that was consummated on the cross of Calvary, [Jesus] took upon himself every sin and sorrow, every heartache and infirmity, every sickness, sadness, trial, tribulation experienced by the children of God from Adam to the end of the world. How he did that is a stunning mystery, but he did it . . . [making] merciful intercession for all the children of men.[8]

Joseph Smith himself gave an orthodox-sounding account of salvific matters on the occasion of the founding of the Church of Christ in April of 1830: "[W]e know," said Joseph, "that all men must repent and believe on the name of Jesus Christ, and worship the Father in his name, and endure in faith on his name to the end, or they cannot be saved in the kingdom of God." And then he added: "And we know that justification through the grace of our Lord and Savior Jesus Christ is just and true; And we know also, that sanctification through the grace of our Lord and Savior Jesus Christ is just and true, to all those who love and serve God with all their mights, minds, and strength" (D&C 20:29–31).

In statements like these we find many classical Christian soteriological expressions. Human beings are fallen and incapable of securing salvation by their own efforts. Only a Savior sent from heaven could save us, and he did so in a redemptive mission that culminated in the atoning sacrifice on the Cross of Calvary.

We can also see in these statements that the more Mormons gravitate toward the language of classical soteriology, the more they also adopt ways of talking about God that echo the classical tradition. It is significant, for example, that in that same 1830 address Joseph articulates a robust doctrine of God: "[W]e know," Joseph says, "that there is a God in heaven, who is infinite and eternal, from everlasting to everlasting the same unchangeable God, the framer of heaven and earth, and all things which are in them" (D&C 20:17).

There is an important topic here, then, for theological discussion, addressing a concern that was expressed nicely by Norman Malcolm, a longtime

---

7. Glenn L. Pearson, *Know Your Religion* (Salt Lake City: Bookcraft, 1961), 169.

8. Jeffrey R. Holland, *Christ and the New Covenant* (Salt Lake City: Deseret Book Company, 1997), 228.

professor at Cornell University who was also a devout Christian, in a discussion of Anselm's ontological argument for God's existence, an argument that purports to show that there must exist "a being than which no greater can be conceived." In the final analysis, Malcolm noted at the end of his rather technical discussion, the interest in establishing the reality of the greatest conceivable Being can only be evaluated properly by attending to the underlying human quest that gives rise to the very idea of such a being. Malcolm explains:

> There is the phenomenon of feeling guilt for something that one has done or thought or felt or for a disposition one has. One wants to be free of this guilt. But sometimes the guilt is felt to be so great that one is sure that nothing one can do oneself, nor any forgiveness by another human being, would remove it. One feels a guilt that is beyond all measure, a guilt "greater than which cannot be conceived." Paradoxically, it would seem, one nevertheless has an intense desire to have this incomparable guilt removed. One requires a forgiveness that is beyond all measure, a forgiveness "greater than which cannot be conceived." Out of such a storm of the soul, I am suggesting, there arises the conception of a forgiving mercy that is limitless, beyond all measure. This is one important feature of the Jewish and Christian conception of God.[9]

This is the struggle of the human soul that Mormons and traditional Christians would do well to discuss together. What does God need to be like in God's "being" in order to save the likes of us? And closely related: What kind of Savior would be needed—in *his* very "being"—to accomplish the redemptive task? Is the gap between human unworthiness and divine mercy that seems to be implicit in so many of Mormonism's own formulations of the human predicament and the greatness of salvation—is that gap capable of being explained adequately by a theology in which the God who saves and the humans who receive that gracious salvation are "of the same species" ontologically?

*****

Now, my second focus: the factors that stimulate the development of doctrine.

Father John Courtney Murray, the great American Jesuit theologian, argued, convincingly in my opinion, that the Nicene formula regarding the "being" of Christ, while certainly moving from the descriptive language of the Bible to a more "ontological mode of conception," was in fact driven by decidedly practical spiritual concerns. In order to preserve the deeply "rela-

---

9. Norman Malcolm's contribution to a symposium on "Contemporary Views of the Ontological Argument," in *The Ontological Argument: From St. Anselm to Contemporary Philosophers*, ed. Alvin Plantinga (Garden City, N.Y.: Anchor Books, 1965), 158.

tional" sense of what the Scriptures say about Jesus, that he is "with us" in our humanity as the Lord of our lives, it was necessary to give a clear expression of what he is "in himself" as the Christ.[10]

The necessity for making this step was the fact of Christological disagreement in the fourth century about the nature of Christ, a reality that simply had to be adjudicated if there was to be a clear and commonly accepted understanding of what it means for Jesus to be the One who "for us and for our salvation . . . came down from heaven." And while the Latter-day Saints presently exempt themselves from that consensus, sticking with, as John Welch put it, "the pure and simple spirit that had prevailed in the apostolic era," it will be interesting to see what happens when the LDS leadership decides that this "pure and simple spirit" is being violated in various Mormon expressions about the person and work of Christ.

My own prediction is that as the scholarly study of Mormon doctrine continues to grow in impressive ways the need for new doctrinal adjudications will become pressing. A case in point for my conviction in that regard is a report in a recent issue of *Sunstone* magazine about a discussion group that met in a Phoenix home on an evening in October 2009. The writer was a participant, and he reports with some enthusiasm the range of views represented in the group, which he characterizes as a gathering of "misfit Mormons." The intellectual "tent was certainly large that evening," he says. "Internet Mormons, Chapel Mormons, Ex-Mormons, Post Mormons, Feminist Mormons, Gay Mormons"—and even, he says, "a couple of Catholics thrown in to add some diversity."[11]

As a longtime subscriber to *Sunstone,* I could have recommended some of *Sunstone*'s other writers who would have added yet more diversity to the mix: Jungian Mormons, Deconstructionist Mormons, Process Theology Mormons, Mormons who sneak off to Anglican services, and so on.

The very existence of an increasingly expanding Mormon intellectual "tent" is a relatively new phenomenon. It is not unthinkable that there may come a time when the LDS church is faced with the need to establish boundaries in how the faithful are to understand—to make clear sense of—"the pure and simple spirit that had prevailed in the apostolic era." My hunch is that that occasion will be very much like a "Nicene moment." But even if my hunch is a mere exercise in wishful thinking, it is a good thing to be talking together about these supremely important matters.

---

10. John Courtney Murray, *The Problem of God* (New Haven, Conn.: Yale University Press, 1964), 46–50.

11. John Wilcox, "Island of the Misfit Mormons," *Sunstone* (March 2010): 12.

The Fundamental Law of Opposition: Lehi and Schelling

by Jad Hatem

In *The Theological Foundations of the Mormon Religion*, Sterling McMurrin considers what I've called the *theorem of Lehi*, according to which there must necessarily be an opposition in all things. McMurrin offers up two possible interpretations: First, evil exists to make good possible such that God creates or allows evils to the favor of a greater good. Related to this is that idea that evil is necessary to experience and appreciate the value of good (an option McMurrin thinks distasteful). A second option is that rather than stipulating that the opposition must exist with a purpose in mind, it is content with observing that evil exists as a matter of metaphysical necessity. Beside the fact that this description lends itself to a dialectical metaphysics (McMurrin mentions Taoism, Heraclitus, Hegel, and Marx), it is conducive with a theodicy that bases its arguments in the limitation of God's power. On this view, God is not responsible for the creation or allowance of evil.

In this article, I defend a scheme that combines the first option (a teleology of evil) with a theme that belongs to the second (divine limitation), which guarantees God's innocence. What is excluded is the idea that evil exists as a matter of fact.[1] My purpose is to integrate Lehi's theorem into a dynamic theodicy that utilizes Friedrich Schelling's dialectic philosophy, and to do so without removing it from its Mormon context. Having already connected points related to the fundamental law of opposition, I would like now to compare Mormon theology with Schelling's *Investigations into the Essence*

---

1. I do not believe that Hegel or Marx believed that evil exists of necessity. But these considerations are beyond the scope of this paper.

of Human Freedom (1809) where the law of opposition appears for the first time, so that I draw the limits of the field where the implementation would be justified.[2] I'll use the words theorem (though it's rather a postulate) and law in order to distinguish them formally.

I'll start from the periphery to get step by step closer to the center where I place the theorem and the law. I'll then proceed with a confrontation.

DOCTRINAL BACKGROUND

Mormon theology has in common with *Of Human Freedom* the fact that neither is in conformity with Christian orthodoxy. As influenced by Luther as Schelling often is, his conception of the nature of God and of His relationship with the world is exterior to the frame drawn by Christianity. There is no question of an Immanent Trinity since the Verb is generated in view of the Creation. Further, God is bestowed with a materiality in that His reason for being, rather than being a simple notion (as in Leibniz), becomes consistent as a dynamic and desiring entity that will offer the universe its raw material. Finally, it does not stand beyond time. He is becoming. These propositions already offer motives of comparison. Mormon theology substitutes a tritheism (at least) to Trinity,[3] and holds that God (or the gods [Elohim]) is bestowed with matter and temporality. The essence of Schelling's post-1797 philosophy of Nature is the acknowledgment of the consistency of reality as a foundation for the ideal. Schelling's innovation in *Of Human Freedom* is to think about God as intratemporal but also as becoming. One could also say that Schelling's God is not that simple since He is compound with his "ground," which guarantees the personality in which "only life is."[4] Likewise, it is well known that Mormon theology's God is composed of parts.[5]

---

2. J. Hatem, *Les Trois Néphites, le Bodhisattva et le Mahdî ou l'ajournement de la béatitude comme acte messianique* (Paris: Ed. du Cygne, 2007), ch. VI.

3. *The Essential Orson Pratt* (Salt Lake City: Signature Books, 1991), 380.

4. Friedrich Wilhelm Joseph Schelling, *Sämmtliche Werke*, 10 vols. (Stuttgart: Cotta, 1856–1861), 7:413. (English translation: Friedrich Willhelm Joseph Schelling, *Investigations into the Essence of Human Freedom*, trans. Jeff Love and Johannes Schmidt [Albany: State University of New York Press, 2006], 74–75. Unless noted, page numbers in parantheses following references to the *Sämmtliche Werke* are for the Love and Schmidt translation.) "God," says Schelling, "is the absolute unity of nature and personality." Friedrich Wilhelm Joseph Schelling, *Philosophische Entwürfe und Tagebücher 1846* (Hamburg: Meiner, 1998), 46. All translations of Schelling in the main text are by the author.

5. James Talmage, *Articles of Faith* (Salt Lake City: The Church of Jesus Christ of Latter-day Saints, 1982), 48; *Essential Orson Pratt*, 79.

The fact that God is not impassible and has human behaviors does not impact either doctrine. Schelling claims anthropomorphism as a consequence.[6] Mormon theology holds that God has a human figure in the image of which man was created (Ether 3:16). It is even the case that—according to one view controversial even among Mormons, though it was taught by Joseph Smith—that God is of human origin,[7] a suggestion that has countless implications. I, however, will focus only on the idea that between man and God there is more than an analogy, there is identity of structure, and a difference due to transformation. Joseph Smith affirms the literal biblical assertion of the creation of Adam in the image of God. He has no need for the expedients of religion that Druzism, Nusayrism, and even orthodox Christianity do. They make God borrow a human figure in order to show Himself to men. God takes on an illusory figure in the first two persons of the Trinity, a real one for the third. But even if Mormon theology admits Incarnation, it preserves God's power to manifest Himself in the shape of man independently from terrestrial flesh, since He personally owns that human shape. Hence it is that the Father appears to Joseph Smith. The convergences with Schelling, then, are the following: man is ipseity and matter, like God. Both of them being spirit, they are solely distinguished by the fact that the link between universal will and particular will is breakable in man (that is the condition of the possibility of evil), whereas it is not in God. They both are the same structure, then, but only in general, because of this decisive difference: whereas Schelling's Absolute becomes progressively human, the Mormon God comes out of humanity.

Although I've used the word creation (and I will continue to do so), it is clear that Mormon theology and Schelling both reject an *ex nihilo* creation. This rejection has an effect on the problem of theodicy, since God cannot be held entirely responsible for what is or appears. Creation is rather a formation from a pre-existent reality, totally distinct from the Demiurge, according to Mormon theology, and relatively distinct according to Schelling.

When it comes to the notion of omnipotence, things are more delicate. Both Schelling's and Mormonism's positions are less certain. Talmage, for instance, defends a doctrine of omnipotence.[8] McMurrin, however, holds a different opinion. He both insists that the Mormon God, who doesn't operate

6. J. Hatem, *De l'Absolu à Dieu* (Paris: Cariscript, 1987), ch. II.

7. "God Himself was once as we are now, and is an exalted man." Joseph Smith, *History of the Church of Jesus Christ of Latter-day Saints,* ed. B. H. Roberts, 7 vols. (Salt Lake City: Deseret Book, 1980), 6:305.

8. Talmage, *Articles of Faith,* 44.

ex nihilo, is not absolute,[9] and that man's free will is assured. His analysis of the problem of theodicy deserves to be quoted here:

> Clearly the three concepts of the absolute goodness of God, the absolute-ness of his power, and the positive reality of evil are not mutually compat-ible as ingredients of a theistic world view. One of them must be compro-mised to save the other two. No cultured religion can sacrifice the first; traditional orthodox Christianity has at times lived with inconsistency and at other times hesitantly sacrificed the third; Mormonism, liberal Protes-tantism, and some philosophical theology have sacrificed the second.[10]

We should agree with McMurrin. Though he does not ignore the theologians' and preachers' use of rhetoric about divine omnipotence, he still holds it to be incompatible with the essence of the doctrine.[11] Schelling's God is no less limited in His power. God creates us using a material cause of which He is not the master. Further, this material cause is not itself created out of noth-ingness; God also uses man's services (the good and less good) to pursue the work of his own revelation. Hence the extraordinary sentence: "Man stands at a crossroads. Whatever he chooses, it will be his act, but he can't remain undecided, because God must necessarily manifest himself, and in creation absolutely nothing equivocal should survive."[12]

Mormon theology and Schelling's theology diverge, however. That seems obvious, insofar as Schelling claims he is a Pantheist, but, according to Mor-mon theology, the things that constitute the world are not modes of God. But this Spinozist characterization of Pantheism, McMurrin notes, is not the only form of Pantheism (and certainly not the form to which Schelling subscribes).[13] Furthermore, the fact that the Mormon God is composed of matter (however subtle) leads, if not to Pantheism as such, at least to a monistic universe that is substantially one. In a way one could claim that the Mormon God is tran-scendent.[14] However, it still seems that He's made of the same substance as the rest of the universe (which is not obvious for Schelling). McMurrin, though, is mistaken in his contrasting Mormonism and Protestantism on these mat-

---

9. Sterling M. McMurrin, *The Theological Foundations of the Mormon Religion* (Salt Lake City: Signature Books, 1965), 27.

10. Ibid., 105.

11. Ibid., 35. In his note about divine omnipotence, David Paulsen specifies that this notion shouldn't be taken in its traditional meaning of unlimited power, a contradictory concept. David L. Paulsen, "Omnipotent God; Omnipresence of God; Omniscience of God," *Encyclopedia of Mormonism,* 4 vols.(Macmillan: New York, 1992), 3:1030.

12. Schelling, *Sämmtliche Werke,* 7:374 (41–42).

13. McMurrin, *Theological Foundations of the Mormon Religion,* 102.

14. Ibid., 9.

ters. Rather than contrasting Mormonism with Lutheranism, and grouping it (Mormonism) with Calvinism, McMurrin should have contrasted Mormonism with paganism. Conceived this way, the distinction between Mormonism and Schelling is a distinction between theomonism (God is everything) and monism (God is part of everything).[15] One must specify that there are as many Pantheisms as there are Monisms. Some are reductive (spiritualist or materialistic for instance). The Monism that should, in my opinion, define Mormon ontology subsumes plurality. However, since God's transcendence is relative, Mormon ontology doesn't contradict Levinas' definition of Paganism as "total impotence of getting out of the world. It doesn't consist in denying spirits and gods, but in placing them in the world,"[16] or, if one prefers, in the immanence of the elements. As enlarged as it can be, the world remains the world. The eternity of souls in Mormonism is of an elemental kind.

COMPARISON

The frame is configured in a way that it must allow the comparison between Lehi's theorem and Schelling's law of opposition. Let us first turn to the texts:

1. What I refer to as the theorem of Lehi is the passage found in 2 Nephi 2:11 and spoken by its first great prophetic figure: "It must needs be, that there is an opposition in all things." The theorem also refers to the following corollary claims: "If not so . . . righteousness could not be brought to pass, neither wickedness, neither holiness nor misery, neither good nor bad. Wherefore all things must needs be a compound in one."

2. In the intermediary period of his intellectual career, Schelling formulates his law in two different places. It occurred first in *Of Human Freedom*, then in the *Stuttgart Lectures* that grant it its name: (a) "Each being can only be revealed in its contrary, love in hate, unity in conflict";[17] (b) "The *fundamental law of opposition*. Without opposition [there is] no life, for man as for every existence in general."[18]

---

15. Something symmetric to Panentheism, thus, theo-en-panism. Note that this doctrine appeared progressively. The Book of Mormon itself shows more respect for divine transcendence.

16. Emmanuel Levinas, *L'Actualité de Maïmonide*, in *Cahier de L'Herne, Emmanuel Lévinas* (Paris: L'Herne, 1991), 144.

17. Schelling, *Sämmtliche Werke*, 7:373 (40–41).

18. Ibid., 7:435 (English translation: Friedrich Willhelm Joseph Schelling, "Stuttgart Seminars," in *Philosophy and the Endgame of Theory: Three Essays by F.W.J. Schelling*, trans. Thomas Pfau [Albany: State University of New York Press, 1994], 208).

Only after announcing the coming of the Messiah and the necessity of judgment does Lehi formulate his theorem. He must explain why judgment envelops punishment and happiness as two opposites, the former having to meet the requisites of atonement. The negation of moral oppositions would lead to that of justice; it would be like denying God's existence. The Book of Alma shows the consequence in striking terms: if the work of justice were destroyed, God would cease to be God (Alma 42:13, 22, 42). Since God is the creator, it is He who must question the existence of the world (2 Ne. 2:13). It is clear that Lehi is not content with merely acknowledging this stubborn, universal, moral, cosmic, and even theological, fact. Instead, he presents it as an explicative principle that gives meaning. Seen this way, it reveals a functioning, but also a finality. It is necessary that things are as such. The Doctrine and Covenants also touches on the subject (but with more authority, since it is held to be God's direct word): "It must needs be that the devil should tempt the children of men, or they could not be agents unto themselves; for if they never should have bitter they could not know the sweet" (D&C 29:39). Once again, the theorem of Lehi is considered as the condition, if not of freedom, at least of its practice. The bitter and the sweet evoke the two fruits of Eden, and must be also understood in a moral sense, rather than a physical one, because the mechanical passage from pain to pleasure and pain again—which is the fate of human existence after the fall—is not linked to any act of freedom. In terms of idea, what precedes evil is the fundamental law of opposition itself that guarantees freedom. Evil doesn't proceed from freedom. The latter is only the place of emergence of evil.[19]

McMurrin has thus taken the path of rational theodicy at the expense of the text's meaning when he chose the explanation of opposition as a raw fact that would leave God safe from any imputation of evil. What is essential is not God, but Life, which includes divinity. After the second corollary, Lehi specifies indeed that if nothing was composed and reduced to a unique body, the latter would have no life, nor sensitivity. When I say that divinity itself is submitted to oppositional polarity I am alluding above all, in the immediate context, to the fall of the angel who becomes a demon because he sought evil before God (2 Ne. 2:17). I am also referring to a doctrine that follows closely doctrines found in the Book of Mormon, according to which Satan sought to deserve to be the Son by atoning for humanity. He demanded to receive the honor of God as a reward (Mosiah 4:1), an honor that, according to Doctrine and Covenants 29:36, is equivalent to divine power.

---

19. Neither Lehi nor Schelling would say that God created Satan out of the transgressions and sins of the believers.

Are we generally aware that Satan pretended to suspend the theorem of Lehi because he wished to save all souls? The text subtly insinuates this by quoting the Father as saying that, besides his rebellion, Satan was also trying to destroy man's free agency (Moses 4:3). Opposition, however, is for Lehi a condition of human freedom: "Wherefore, the Lord God gave unto man that he should act for himself. Wherefore, man could not act for himself save it should be that he was enticed by the one or other" (2 Ne. 2:16). This point calls to mind the two trees in Paradise. They have become here symbols of the double postulation.

An irony in the Book of Moses is an unexpected project embarked upon by Satan: instead of canceling opposition, he reinforces it and emphasizes it. He reinforces opposition by making tangible the contrast latent between Christ (the true Son, as the Father insists) and Satan. He emphasizes opposition insofar as it is a secret desire of opposition (to the Father at first, but perhaps also to the Son) that encourages his candidacy. The power of reality is such that any maneuver must take opposition into consideration. The good could not neglect the law of opposition out of idealism, because not only would it fail miserably, it would also provoke as a backlash a renewal of evil. It is obvious that the reciprocal is true: an excess in evil brings upon a renewed good. Jung has granted this law the name of *enantiodromia*, which means running in an opposite direction.[20]

However, this convocation of the opposite keeps a mechanical and external character as long as the opposites are not revealed one in another. Not only is one felt by contrast with the other as the sweet and the sour, but one comes about through the other, which makes Schelling's interest in this question so important.

It is possible, it seems to me, to distinguish four states of the law of opposition. I will begin with the inferior one:

1. *The coexistence of contraries.* Things are mixed. This notion is referred to by Lehi in 2 Nephi. Giordano Bruno illustrates the notion as well: "Nothing is pure and simple . . . ; all things are made of contraries; and as a result of this composition, which is at the heart of things, the affections that attach us to it do not lead us to any enjoyment that would not be mixed with some bitterness."[21] We recognize here the theorem of Lehi and its second corollary. For Lehi, however, it is good and necessary that things are submitted to composition, and

---

20. Carl Jung, *Psychological Types: The Collected Works of C. G Jung, Vol. 6*, trans. H. G. Baynes (Princeton, N.J.: Princeton University Press, 1976), 709.

21. Giordano Bruno, *Des Fureurs héroïques*, I, II (Paris : Les Belles Lettres, 1954), 158.

that alters the perspective. Bruno himself prefers the middle region where the extremes cancel each other out.[22]

2. *The reciprocal determination of contraries through the negative way.* Bruno continues: "And even more: if bitterness weren't a part of things, enjoyment wouldn't be there either, since it is tiredness that makes us find rest enjoyable." It is not by itself that a word is present to another, but by its absence, which meets the theory of the least degree. Bruno takes the risk here of introducing the notion of causality: "If we observe closely, we would always find that a contrary is a cause for the other contrary to wake desire, and for it to please." But this law of contrasts only expresses a causality by default, which the first corollary of the theorem of Lehi doesn't encourage us to admit, since it places the stake directly at the level of morals and salvation and it does so in a way that for him implies freedom.

3. *The reciprocal determination of the contraries through the positive way.* Wherein this statement of the law of opposition causality is active and the law is truly dynamic. What is essential for Lehi is that the theorem must ensure the foundation of freedom. Without duality there is no choice; and without duality of opposition there is no ethical or religious choice. This falls out of the fact that there is only a matter of choice of a term as *against* another, something that Schelling has perfectly conceived, since for him struggle is the main element of life, and evil must be awakened in order to be overcome.[23]

It is thanks to this polarity that the spark of life is communicated to the whole being. The second corollary redounds on the theorem and explains it, transplanting it from the first state of the law to the third one. But Schelling's theory includes an extra element, which leads us to consider a fourth state of the law of opposition.

4. *The reciprocal determination of the contraries through a positive way as a revelation of each.* Lehi supposes that good and evil are known. This is problematic, since the frontier between them is blurry. First, they must be defined. Then, one needs to be sure that one is not mistaken for the other. There are still more subtle confusions. It is sometimes held, for instance, that the better is the enemy of good. This would mean the good has two enemies, evil and that excess of good that could very well, out of an unwilling enantiotropy, convoke the evil that it is not.

---

22. Ibid., 162.
23. Schelling, *Sämmtliche Werke*, 7:400 (63–64).

Even if Schelling's reflection considers these issues, for him the essential point comes at an earlier stage and concerns the manifestation of good and evil. Love demands hate as an opposite in order to be effective,[24] which amounts to the claim that it remains latent within what stands facing it (*Gegenteil*). Indeed, love as a simple disposition is hardly more than impotency. That *hardly more* is important because it is a lever. At rest, however, it is a promise of accomplishment. If it is to be accomplished, though, it must lack the element of struggle, mentioned above. To truly appear (appear in this instance means to be), it must win over an adverse force. But the latter is not inert, as if evil were a defect of good, a hole in the being, the resistance of a matter or the end of an effort. It must have the status of facing. Hatred is not indifference. Hatred searches for love in order to bring it down. Hatred would be timid if it didn't find love, which is why it happens that evil can provoke the good, not only afterwards because of *enantiodromy*, but beforehand, in order to accomplish itself as evil or gain the supreme degree. It is said that Gilles de Rais, the greatest criminal of all time, imagined a scenario in which he would try to get his child victims to love him before he stabbed them.[25] Evil is the place of the revelation of the good.

Schelling agrees with Lehi: there can't be good or evil without opposition to justice or to holiness. This makes freedom and retribution possible. But the philosopher goes further than the prophet in that he conceives man's freedom as the act by which good and evil become what they are. It is not only the choice between two realities that is at stake, but their coming into being. For states of being that are in opposition, and so stand ready to reveal one *in another*, the fight should not be led only against indifference. Hatred should be its peak, its maximum of auto-manifestation, as hatred of love, the very thing that should be vanquished. It is appropriate that Christ insists that the sin against the Holy Spirit cannot be atoned for. Indeed, this sin is tantamount to declaring that the Man of Nazareth heals by the power of the devil. Is it not to claim that the good is evil, and by that to attempt to give a fatal blow to the good? That is how the good and the evil are opposed to banality and must confront each other. This theme is prominent in the Book of Mormon, even when not underscored by Lehi's theorem.

In the blasphemous equation, the good is the evil, the copula is understood in its analytical sense. The same equation can be found in Schelling's text where he expresses its dialectical value. Good is evil means that the good is the foundation of evil—in other words, evil doesn't have by itself the power

---

24. Ibid., 7:374 (41–42).

25. Jad Hatem, *L'Echarde du mal dans la chair de Dieu* (Paris: Cariscript, 1987), ch. III, § 7.

of being.[26] But the philosopher only formulates the equation to express the copula as such. The idea itself, of good being the subject of evil, is Thomist. Schelling uses the expression in a context that is particular to him, when he claims that "evil and good are the same, simply looked upon from different aspects, or also that evil is, in itself, at the roots of its identity, the good, as the good would be, on another hand, when it's considered in its scission or non-identity, evil."[27] Not that these two realities can be confused of course, but they are only distinguished by their form. Good and evil combine differently the universal will and the particular will that are found in all things. In the good, the former prevails over the latter, and it's the reverse in evil, which makes of it a perversion rather than a privation of good. Instead of repeating that cold and heat could only be felt through contrast, Schelling claims something totally different, that cold can only be felt because the body includes the root of heat.[28] In other words, besides the fact that the body is susceptible to opposites, this means that those opposites are composed of the same ingredients. The difference is in their arrangement—even if this arrangement is determined by an element that comes from outside the other root.[29] From the dialectical identity of good and evil, Schelling comes to the conclusion that whoever doesn't hold in himself the energy of evil is equally incapable of good,[30] which confirms that the good is not less apt to fight than evil.

GOD AND OPPOSITION

When Lehi says that there must necessarily be an opposition in all things, he doesn't exclude anyone. As God is submitted explicitly by Leibniz to the principle of reason, He is implicitly submitted by Lehi to the law of opposition. I have already invoked the opposition in divinity that emerges at the moment of rivalry between Lucifer and Christ. This move reflects a rivalry between the Father and the insidious candidate for divinity. This moment requests a new argument. Mormon doctrine claims God's mutability. But God cannot do without internal and external opposition. The suggestions I have been making hold some promise for solving the controversy among Mormon theologians regarding whether God is changeless or dependent on dynamic perfection. My claim here is that the theorem of Lehi encourages the second hypothesis. One can of course imagine many things about the nature of opposition *in* God. It might, for instance, be a sexual type (as in

---

26. Schelling, *Sämmtliche Werke*, 7:342 (14).

27. Ibid., 7:400 (63–64).

28. Ibid..

29. Ibid., 7:370 (38).

30. Ibid., 7:400 (63–64).

the Kabbalah). The most reasonable consideration, though, would be to ask Schelling, for whom God originates from the Groundless. The Groundless, being non-difference, doesn't admit opposition as such, but it could still contain distinct principles that would only be opposed in their manifested state.[31] Evil for instance is latent in the absolute as a possibility, and only rises in being to be eternally overcome. And the good, as latent, only becomes good by overcoming, through which the opposite force that has become sub-placed, and is maintained as raw material for any process. Take, for instance, the following example from the *Stuttgart Lectures*: God raises one of the principles that constitute him, selfishness, above the other, love, in a way that a creation becomes possible without putting in danger the existence of God, since selfishness, which expresses ipseity, must be preserved.[32] If selfishness had dominated love, God would be inversed; rather than Pantheism, Pandemonism would have reigned! It is in this context that Schelling writes:

> For the ordinary, abstract mode of understanding, it seems surprising that God should contain a non-divine principle, without consciousness and lesser than He. To conceive God as an empty identity, however, is not to comprehend Him at all. The necessity of this hypothesis can be proven by means of the *fundamental law of opposition*. Without opposition no life, for man as for every existence in general.[33]

The Absolute must itself go through separation and opposition so that life makes its shining apparition. But Schelling's God aspires throughout history to be all in all,[34] in a way that all oppositions are appeased. If opposition is a fact of being, as Lehi claims it is, then it is understandable that no accomplishment can put an end to it (opposition). If opposition were an element of revelation, as Schelling purports, we shall admit easily that we can hope it will lose its acuity in proportion as the mystery will be elucidated. This is to say that love will reign. "The groundless divides itself into two equally eternal beginnings only in order for the two which could not be in it as groundless at the same time or be one there, should become one through love; that it divides itself only so that there may be life, love and personal existence."[35] We understand that hatred must be first manifested. God, however, is not directly capable of the power of good and evil. This renders God relatively impotent, but oh, how reassuring this impotence is! On the scission and aspiration for union, the young Schelling of the *Introduction to an Outline of a System of*

---

31. Ibid., 7:407 (69).
32. Ibid., 7:439 (Schelling, "Stuttgart Seminars," 210–11).
33. Ibid., 7:436 (Schelling, "Stuttgart Seminars," 208).
34. Ibid., 7:408 (69–70).
35. Ibid.

Philosophy of Nature, wrote some inspired, and appropriate, lines. Although they concern nature, I daresay that they are also applicable to God and to the fundamental law of opposition:

> Nature is the *most lazy beast* and it loathes separation, for it is the only thing that forces it to be active; it is only active in order to get rid of this constraint. Opposites must eternally run away from each other to eternally search for each other, and eternally search for each other so that they never find each other. It is only in *this* contradiction that resides the foundation of the activity of all of nature.[36]

---

36. Ibid., 3:325.

Dwelling in Hope

by James E. Faulconer

Obviously hope is central to Christian understanding. Pauline and post-Pauline New Testament writings understand hope as hope in the resurrection of Christ, made manifest in the Second Coming (e.g., Acts 24:15 and 1 Thess. 2:19). The Book of Mormon use of the term seems somewhat more broad, though closer analysis might show that the New Testament understanding is equally broad. In any case, the Book of Mormon speaks of hope for the restoration of Israel (e.g., 1 Ne. 19:24), hope for salvation (e.g., Alma 58:11), and hope for the glory of Christ (e.g., Jacob 4:4), which in context could refer either to the First or the Second Coming. I assume that an investigation of the various ways that the scriptures use the word *hope* would be profitable. But my interest here is in giving a brief phenomenology of hope rather than a scriptural account of it. My assumption is that if I succeed, what I say might help us hear the scriptural discussion of hope with new ears.

Of course there may not be only one thing that we call hope. It is not difficult to imagine that there is, at best, only a family resemblance between the various ways that we use the word and that there is more than one phenomenon that we call hope. If so, the description of hope that I offer will be one that chooses its examples from everyday life with an eye on the phenomenon of religious hope. Rather than defining hope *per se*, I will describe ordinary hope as broadly as possible in a way that I believe helps us better understand scriptural hope.

The first thing to notice is that hope is a state of belief, a belief that something is possible. It is incoherent to say that I hope for rain, but I do not believe it is possible. At the same time, it is equally impossible to hope for rain if I am certain that it will rain. Hope is for something that is possible but not certain; a person who hopes does not confuse her hopes with certainties. Hope knows that what it hopes for is, to some degree, improbable, perhaps highly improbably, perhaps not.

What about something that I expect? Can I hope for that? Can I only hope for the improbable and not also for the probable? What about cases such as "I hope the basketball team wins tomorrow night," when they are playing a team that I reasonably believe they will beat? Is this real hope or is it just a way of speaking? Can I only hope for what I understand to be improbable? I think not.

Hoping for the basketball team to win when I expect them to win shows that hope recognitizes that things do not always go as we reasonably expect them to. It is as if I say, "I expect the team to win because I believe they will and because I have good reasons for my belief. Nevertheless, I know that there is always a chance that they will not and, in the face of that possibility, I hope they will win." Such cases are interesting because they confirm that hope recognizes some improbability *regardless* of degree. The improbability that I recognize need not be greater than the probability—though it often and perhaps usually, is—but if I hope, I recognize that what I hope for is, to some degree or in some sense, improbable. This allows me to offer a rough distinction between hope and expectation: hope focuses on the improbability of an event, though it may also recognize its probability; expectation has its focus on probability and takes the improbability to be relatively insignificant.

It also seems that hope is always for a good. Of course, there is a sense in which I can hope for what is bad, recognizing that it is bad. We can imagine an angry person sincerely saying, "I ought not to kill someone's pet, but I hope that, when the poison I have ordered arrives by mail, I will still want to kill my neighbor's barking dog." In spite of recognizing that his desire is bad, such a person sees the death of his neighbor's dog as something desirable—as *a* good though not *the* good. Structurally hope is an existential commitment to the possibility of a, perhaps relative, good that recognizes some degree of improbability of that good.

At the same time, hope is a species of humility, for hope recognizes that the good I hope for is ultimately beyond my control. I hope because I am a finite being; an infinitely powerful being could not hope since any object of his or her desire would in principle be achievable. On my analysis, the fact that hope is a recognition of our finitude will turn out to be the key to understanding it.

Christian philosophers have understood hope as something necessarily future-oriented.[1] As a result, Josef Pieper, following the tradition, describes natural hope as a function of youth: the young have a longer future than the old, so they can be more hopeful.[2] In contrast, the rebirth of Christian conversion gives one a new temporality and, so, renews hope, making it possible even for those who are no longer naturally young. I do not deny the distinction between natural hope and the hope that comes with Christian rebirth. It is a helpful distinction. However, with Spinoza, I will argue that it is a mistake to assume that either natural or Christian hope is necessarily oriented to the future.

Unlike Christian thinkers, Spinoza doesn't insist on the future orientation of hope. To see the problem with understanding hope as only future-oriented, consider the statement, "I hope I didn't break my leg." The standard view is that hopes like that must be explained as future-oriented, even though they appear, at first glance, to be oriented to the past. On this view, if I hope that I didn't break my leg, then I know that it is already broken or it is not—but I hope it will turn out that it is not. Thus, if hope is necessarily future-oriented, the hope that my leg is not broken is not so much a hope with regard to my leg as it is a hope for what I will in the future learn about what has already happened. To hope regarding what happened in the past is to confess my ignorance about the past and to hope to learn something in the future.

Although Spinoza doesn't believe that hope is necessarily future-oriented, he agrees that it is an epistemic state, a particular kind of self-consciousness of ignorance. He says, "Hope is an inconstant pleasure, which has arisen from the idea of a thing that is present or past, about whose outcome we are in some doubt."[3] Both for religious Aquinas and a-religious Spinoza hope remains only an epistemic matter. That means that what appears in Spinoza to be hope directed at the past is really hope about a future epistemic state. But the reduction of hope to an epistemic state, ignorance, also doesn't work.

Consider other cases that show the problem. For example, "I hope that my friend did not suffer when she died" or a parent's response, "I should hope not," when a child brags, "I didn't cheat on the examination." It is unreasonable to insist that hopes like these express desires that I will someday find out that she didn't suffer or that he didn't cheat. I hope that my friend *didn't* suffer or that my child *didn't* cheat on the examination; my intention is directed toward the past event of her suffering or my child's cheating rather than toward the future

---

1. See Thomas Aquinas, *Summa Theologica*, II.II.161.1; and Ernst Bloch, *The Principle of Hope, Vol. 1*, trans. Neville Plaice, Stephen Plaice, and Paul Knight (Cambridge: MIT Press, 1996), 11.

2. Josef Pieper, *Über die Hoffnung* (München: Kösel, 1949), 43. See also Aquinas, I.II.40.1.

3. Baruch Spinoza, *Ethics*, Part III: Definitions of Emotions, 12.

events of me learning about those past events. My hope is for a state of affairs that obtained in the past or should have obtained in the past, *regardless* of what I will or will not find out about that state of affairs. Of course, learning that she suffered or that he cheated will dash my hopes, but hope is not necessarily a desire to know something, nor is it necessarily future-oriented. It is a desire for a state of affairs to obtain, whether in the past or the future.

Why, then, does it seem so natural to assume that hope is future oriented? Presumably this is because of its focus on possibility and our assumption that possibility is a matter of the future. But the past, too, must be understood in terms of possibility. Let me use Heidegger's thought to outline an argument for that claim. Consider his discussion of having-been as repetition,[4] with its clear but implicit reference to Kierkegaard's little book, *Repetition*: if we understand what has been as a by-gone given, as no longer possible, then we cannot truly understand what it means to repeat what happened before. The concept of genuine repetition, doing what has been done before, requires that the past be understood in terms of possibility. If I do what another did in the past, either I merely imitate what he did—which is not what he did, since he wasn't imitating himself—or I do something that repeats the same possibility that he was enacting.

Kierkegaard's question is, "How is repetition of a past event—for example, the repetition of Peter's response to the Christ's call, 'Follow me' (Matthew 4:19)—possible as genuine repetition rather than mere imitation?" Peter did something when he responded to Jesus beside the lake. I want to respond to Jesus as Peter did. The problem is that I know who Jesus was, I know about Peter's response, and I know something of what happened to Peter and, indeed, to the world because of Peter's response. Any response I make to Jesus is conditioned by the response that Peter made. But Peter's response was not conditioned in that way at all. Thus, when I respond, I seem to be doing something very different than Peter did. I seem only to be imitating Peter rather than doing what Peter did, since he wasn't imitating anyone. Does that mean it is impossible for me or any other person in the early twenty-first century to respond fully to Jesus as Peter did? That's what Kierkegaard wants to know—and surely the Christian answer to that question is "no." Heidegger's response to Kierkegaard's question is his understanding of temporality: genuine repetition is only possible if the past is not only something given, but also something open.

To consider the implications of that response, detour for a bit to think about how we usually understand possibility. For ordinary understanding, we have a determinate past that has created the present and, within that present, we

---

4. *Weiderholung*. See Martin Heidegger, *Being and Time*, trans. John Macquarrie and Edward Robinson (San Francisco: Harper Collins, 1962), 387–89.

await the future. The past consists of a set of possibilities that have come to pass and are now fixed, over-and-done. The present is the set of possibilities that can still come about. The future consists of a set of possibilities that will yet come to pass, that are not yet possible but will be, the possibilities that we await to arise as possibilities from the particular possibilities we have at the moment.

In each case ordinary understanding takes the past, present, and future to be a set containing particular determinate elements, namely determinate possibilities. In the case of the past, certain of those possibilities have been realized so the others are no longer actualizable. The past is a set of actualized possibilities. The unactualized possibilities that might have once been part of the chains of events no longer are, having been eliminated when the past possibilities were realized. In the case of the present, the possibilities exist as a determinate set, waiting to be realized, like various links lying about ready to be added to the chain.

The possibilities that constitute the set of future events are, we might say, second order because the present possibilities must be realized (literally "enacted") before future ones can come into being as real possibilities. In turn, each way of realizing the present set of possibilities will result in its own set of future possibilities. For the future as well as the past and present, though knowing the future possibilities would be infinitely more complex, an all-knowing being could know the particular contents of all of those implicate sets. Such a being could know all of the possible chains of events. The future is a perhaps infinitely large, but determinate set of sets, each of them also determinate. Putting the sets of possibilities into the flow of temporality complicates matters, but that complication does not affect my conclusion: possibility is understood in terms of sets of determinate entities. The chain of events is not necessarily determined, but it is determinate. Each actualized possibility determines the next set of possibilities from which something will be actualized *ad infinitum*.

Determination is a problem for understanding free human acts, but so is determinateness: even if the set of possibilities were infinite, *as a set* (in other words, as something with determinate elements) it does not have openness as such. That is what it means to be determinate. The brackets around a set tell us something. They tell us what things are contained within the set and what things are excluded, even if the list of things within the set is infinitely long. The brackets close the set off. A set of infinite possibilities is still a set of these things and not those. It is not open as such. This is equally true of past, present, *and* future when thought of as a set of possibilities. In each case, what they can be is *already given*, even if not yet known—or, for that matter, knowable.

Let me expand on this point since it is the hinge of my argument: there are three ways of understanding possibility. On the first, there is, in reality, no such thing as possibility. The events that occur are causally related to each other in such a way that there is only one set of events. Some of those have come to pass. Some have not yet come to pass. However, the events that will occur are already given, and we have only one way through them. We are generally ignorant of those events except as they occur, so it appears that something could be otherwise than it is—that there is possibility—but that appearance is only an illusion created by ignorance. On this view, things are the way they are and could be no other way: determinism.

The second way is that there is a set of possibilities that are causally related to each other, but they exist in such a way that there are various paths through them, possible decision trees in that already existing set of possibilities. However, to speak of this as a set containing possibilities is still to say that those possibilities already exist. Some have been actualized, some have not, but all exist as elements of the set. Since temporality is irrelevant to the constitution of the set, the actualization of this or that element in the set of possibilities doesn't change the set itself.

It is true that at any moment some or all of the possibilities in the set have not been actualized—and some may never be—but they are nevertheless already given as elements of the set in question. I will refer to this kind of possibility as "potentiality." If we understand possibility as potentiality, then freedom consists in the ability genuinely to choose one path over another within the given potential. I think this is probably the most common way that people understand possibility and freedom.

A third way to understand possibility is as openness *per se*. Often potentiality and openness are taken to be the same thing, but that is a mistake. The difference between the potential and the open is an ontological difference: the potential exists as a property of things, a set of actualizable events that attaches to the thing or to groups of things. A cup has the potential to hold water because it has the property of "open-ended container." In turn, that physical property gives rise to another set of properties: the cup can be used for drinking hot chocolate, holding pencils in it, catching the spider crawling on my desk, etc.

In contrast, the open exists in the way of being of things. This thing I hold in my hand has come to be as stuff[5] in the world opens itself up in the world in some particular way. Stuff reveals itself or is revealed. All revelation of a thing entails content, but it does not entail the actualizing of a property already inherent in the stuff that is. We can say that the difference between

---

5. I use the Anglo-Saxon word *stuff* precisely because of its generic meaning "equipment, stores, stock, materials": that which is before it has been determined as a this or a that.

potentiality and openness is that the former has content—is a set containing elements—and the latter is not a content, but openness to content.

Before saying more about what I mean by openness, reconsider the observation that we usually understand possibility as either determinism or potentiality rather than openness, and let me point to a problem with doing so. Consider the way that religious people in biblical traditions appear to have almost always thought (theologically) about divine foreknowledge: the future exists in some determinate form, whether that of determinism or potentiality. That is what makes it possible for God to know it, though we cannot. However, even if the future exists as a potentiality that God knows completely, a potentiality that only becomes actual in history, for God the possible future exists as this set of determinate and fully cognized possibilities, for which there is ultimately no alternative. Nothing is possible for him since everything is actual, but if nothing is possible for God, then possibility is merely an illusion that humans cannot avoid. Though our temporality may make belief in possibility inescapable, it is nevertheless without ultimate ground. In such a scenario the future is determined, even if not yet determined in time.

Of course, one could say that from the point of view of a being outside of time, the future is both determinate and potential—or neither, take your pick. But each is equally non-sensical. The illusory character of human agency for such an understanding of divine knowledge is a *reductio ad absurdum* for the view. Given the pervasive influence of traditional Christian theology, Latter-day Saints often continue to think in those terms, even if we do not believe in that god. But I cannot see anyway for LDS theology to include the three beliefs (1) that God is embodied, (2) that he exists outside of time and knows every future event in the future, and (3) that human beings are free. The three are incompatible.

To return to the discussion of possibility: the overall point is that ordinary understanding thinks possibility either by denying it as real or by reducing it to the form of determination that I am calling *potentiality*, which also turns out to deny that possibility is real. Ernst Bloch offers an additional argument against both possibility as determination and possibility as potentiality. He does so in a way that sheds additional light on our understanding of hope, and he points to an understanding of possibility as openness that is compatible with the argument that we must think hope in terms of openness. Bloch argues that if what-is is already given—whether as determined or as potential—then actual being is always merely something unfinished and deficient rather than something possible.[6] We assume that the end has already been given, so actual being is always something short of that end until we reach the

---

6. Bloch, *The Principle of Hope*, 18.

end of time. But even at that apocalyptic moment, if what-is is already given, we have been underway only toward the renewal or actualization of what was *already given* in the past. Anything less than a fullness of the given is deficient, so as long as we have not yet come to the end of history, considered as a whole the actual (being less than what is given) is necessarily deficient. Bloch's argument is that the usual view of hope makes the present perpetually deficient and it makes hope for its fulfillment in the end impossible since we cannot genuinely hope for what it is already given.

It follows that only if what-is is *not* already given can we have a genuine as opposed to deficient present and future. According to Bloch, a notion of hope that assumes possibility as openness is central to any attempt to understand the world and human existence that does not assume that actual existence is deficient.[7] Conversely, to repeat, a world in which possibility is merely potentiality is both a deficient world and a world in which hope is impossible except as inescapable illusion. However, the necessity of openness for a non-deficient actual world in which hope is possible means that hope is possible only for those who seek utopia—the fullness of a present that was *not* already-given. Those who hope do not languish in nostalgia for an Edenic past, the already-given, where the most that can occur is the actualization of existing potentiality. The not-yet-revealed future for which we labor rather than the already-given past that we seek to constitute makes hope possible. Structurally hope is necessarily eschatological.

Interestingly, because Bloch sees Christianity as a religion of hope, which he takes to be future-oriented, and because he sees Marx as the only philosopher for whom the future is real, Bloch argues that Marx is the only Christian philosopher. The (fallacious and historically inaccurate) argument looks something like this: Until Marx, philosophers posited the real as already given (in, for example, Platonic forms or the mind of God). As a result, philosophy could not take seriously the idea of the future and the new; it defused hope. Only Marx and Christianity take hope (i.e., the new) seriously, and they understand it in much the same terms. So, according to Bloch, Marx is a Christian philosopher in spite of himself.[8] Of course, this is an instance of an undistributed middle term.

---

7. As I think this paper implies, I believe it is true that we cannot understand consciousness without understanding hope, but not because consciousness is future-oriented (as Bloch argues, ibid., 7). Instead, it is true because consciousness is oriented to possibility.

8. See ibid., 17–18. If I am right about the orientation of consciousness to openness rather than the future (see note 13 of this essay), then it remains to be seen to what degree we can understand Marx in terms of possibility rather than merely the potentiality of the future.

In spite of mistaking Marx for a Christian philosopher, Bloch shows us that the alternative to possibility as determination or possibility as potentiality is genuine openness: the world is open, a field in which things happen rather than a set of potentials to be actualized. On this view, to be a thing is to be an on-going center of manifold events, but there is no *set* of the possible, either as determined or as potential, that contains all of the events that may occur in time. The conclusion about God's foreknowledge that we came to earlier follows here as well: absolute foreknowledge of the future doesn't exist because there's no-thing in the future to know except those based on the events of which the knower is the agent.

We should understand our relation to time as a relation to openness rather than as a relation to some degree of determination. What is perhaps surprising is that this is as true of the past as it is of the present and the future, but this is the claim that will help us better understand what openness means. To say that the past is open goes so much against common sense that it sounds ridiculous. What can we make of that claim that doesn't justify the Thracian maiden's charge against Thales that philosophy is useless star-gazing? I was born in 1947. That is a fact that cannot change. I cannot choose to have been born at another time nor can events bring it about that I was born at some other time. If not, however, what sense does it make to say that past events are open?

I will begin my defense of that understanding of the past by quoting a pregnant clause from Heidegger's essay "Anaximander's Saying": "We think out of the eschatology of being, so we must learn . . . to think the former out of what is here."[9] The past has its being in the present, where it exists as what Hans-Georg Gadamer calls *Wirkungsgeschichtlichebewußtsein*, our consciousness (explicit or otherwise) of the effects of the past—what we can also call *significance*, following Gadamer's usage. The past exists as its present significance, the effects in the present of past events. Since this is as true of things as it is of persons, *Wirkungsgeschichtlichesein*, effective-historical-being, might be a better term than effective-historical-consciousness. Presumably it also makes sense to speak of the effects of the future on our being in the present, to understand those effects as the way in which the future exists. So both the past and the future are their significance in the present, and that significance (the effects of the past and the future) includes the openness of present events and things. The present is the openness of the past and the future in the present.

---

9. My translation. The full sentence is: "Denken wir aus der Eschatologie des Seins, dann müssen wir eines Tages das Einstige der Frühe im Einstigen des Kommenden erwarten und heute lernen, das Einstige von da her zu bedenken." Martin Heidegger, "Der Spruch des Anaximander," *Holzwege* (1946), 302.

That is significance, but for an event to be open is not for it to point to or signify just this or that particular interpretation. Any particular interpretation of an event is a consequence of the possibility of signification. The significance/openness of the event is its malleability, its ability to be other than it is. Openness is signification *per se*.

Thus, significance is not merely a subjective property that individuals add to events and objects. Their significance usually, perhaps always, thrusts itself on us. We do not assign an event or object significance; it *has* significance. Perhaps better: it *is* significance. In addition, the more something has no significance, the less it makes sense to speak of that phenomenon as something at all. It is meaningless to speak of an event or object with absolutely no significance, as if it could exist without any openness at all. Thus the answer to Kierkegaard's question is that genuine repetition repeats the significance of the event. If I merely imitate Peter's response to Jesus, then I am not doing what Peter did. But I can repeat the signification of that event and, in doing so, do what Peter did. However, since the significance of the event is its openness, that is possible only if the past remains open as to its significance, in other words as to its effects in the present. To repeat what someone did in the past is to take up the significance of the world "in the same way," not to do the same thing in some merely physicalistic sense.[10]

This discussion of possibility does not change the earlier description I gave of hope:

1. Hope has belief as a component.
2. In hope one is oriented to a good as possible.
3. One is oriented toward that good as, to some degree, improbable.
4. Bringing that good to pass is not fully in one's power, if at all.

However, this understanding does change our understanding of the second point by showing us the need to rethink possibility: hope is an orientation to possibility, to the openness of events, rather than to the future.

Notice, however, that this rethinking of the second criterion allows us to see that the second and the fourth criteria overlap: to be oriented to possibility-as-such is to be oriented to my finitude. To say, "I hope that my friend did not suffer when she died," is to recognize that her suffering is not only beyond my epistemic ken, it is beyond my control though not beyond my relation to it as open, not beyond significance. My present desire for the good in the past (or fear of the absence of that good) is interrupted by the openness of the past,

---

10. Of course, we must ask whether such a repetition is possible. It seems, however, that Kierkegaard is right: the repetition of significance is ultimately only possible if we have a notion of eternity. How to think that notion of eternity—and whether we can *think* it at all—remains a question.

though I nevertheless continue to desire it as a possible past in the present. I am finite, and my finitude makes hope possible. Given the openness of the past and future in the present, in hope I encounter that openness as oriented toward a good that has significance.

It is important to understand the interruption of my desire by the openness of time in terms of my earlier discussion of openness rather than in traditional terms of not having access to some existing potentiality, an existing set of possibilities. I am not a finite being because a particular determinate possibility has already been given but something prevents me from knowing it or responding to it (the assumption that grounds the explanation of mere epistemic hope) or because something prevents it from coming to actuality. I am a finite being because not everything is given; what-is (past, present, and future) remains open. A totally determined being has no limits because there is nothing outside the totality of which that being is part. Nothing is not-given for such a being.

As I've already suggested, this way of understanding possibility has implications for how we understand the Divine. Nietzsche was right that however much we wish to, we cannot escape metaphysics. But he was also right to declare against the traditional god of metaphysics and to urge us to think in ways that might be disruptive of our passion for metaphysics. The god of traditional metaphysics cannot hope, and for the same reasons the world is not open for such a god.[11] Nothing can interrupt the desire or will of the metaphysically omniscient god because for him there is nothing more than what is, nothing beyond the given, probably nothing other than himself. There is no outside, so he finds himself always within what has been given. There is nothing other to open up possibility, so in the technical sense of the word *infinite* such a being is infinite. He is without limits. But the absence of limits, of something genuinely other, of openness, means that such a being also cannot be free, cannot be a person—or if there is some sense in which he is a person, he must be an autistic, solipsistic person. That isn't the God of the Old Testament, the New Testament, or the Book of Mormon. Christianity has not believed in that god, but not infrequently philosophy and theology have.

At first glance, a human being in a determined or merely potential world would seem to be exactly the opposite of an infinite being. The irony is that such a human being and the god who lives outside of every world are more

---

11. As much of Paul Ricoeur's work demonstrates, however, it is important to recognize that religion need not be unproblematically metaphysical. For a helpful discussion of the relation of philosophical reflection to religion, see Ben Vedder, "The Question into Meaning and the Question of God," *Transcendence in Philosophy and Religion* (Bloomington: Indiana University Press, 2003), 35–53. My intuition is that Mormonism is particularly disposed against metaphysical religion.

alike than one might suppose. Neither is limited. Limitation requires that there be something beyond the limit, something other. But if the world is not open, then there is nothing beyond—no excess, no other—for either a being in a determined world or one in a potential world. Without openness, there is neither restraint nor its absence. Beings in a determinate or in a potential world are unfortunately infinite beings. In contrast, openness means finitude.

Understanding hope as an orientation to possibility and finitude rather than merely to the future is unlikely to change drastically the traditional Christian understanding of hope. Thinkers like Pieper speak of the new life that Christian rebirth brings as a new youthfulness. As our hymn, "If You Could Hie to Kolob" reminds us, for the Christian "There is no end to youth."[12] But we can understand youth not just in terms of having an infinite future, but equally well in terms of new possibilities, or in terms of re-newed possibilities.[13] Indeed, to understand repentance, the promise that one's sins can be wiped away, is to understand hope in terms not only of the possibilities of the future but the renewed possibilities of the past, the re-newed past.

One finds a similar connection of youthfulness and renewed possibilities rather than a renewed future in contemporary science. As the historian of science, Hans-Jörg Rheinberger says,

> Being young . . . is not a result of being located near zero on the time scale; it is a function—if you will—of the very functioning of the system. The age of the system is measured by its capacity to produce differences that count as unprecedented and keep the machinery going.[14]

Understanding hope as an orientation toward possibility rather than as some form of givenness is not a minor shift in understanding.

What might this analysis of hope suggest for our understanding of hope in the scriptures? The answer would be a much longer paper, but I can suggest some things. The first follows from the initial description of hope: to hope for the restoration of Israel, for salvation, and for the presence or glory of Christ is to be oriented in the world in a way such that one believes these things can come to pass and, at the same time, recognizes the objective improbability that

---

12. William W. Phelps, "If You Could Hie to Kolob," *Hymns of the Church of Jesus Christ of Latter-day Saints* (Salt Lake City: Deseret Book, 1985), 284.

13. How much thinking in terms of possibility rather than the Apocalypse would change Christian understanding remains a question. I have suggested that it need not make a large difference, especially if, as I would suggest, one understand the Apocalypse not as simply something to come, but as the limit of our subjectivity and history.

14. Hans-Jörg Rheinberger, *Toward a History of Epistemic Things: Synthesizing Proteins in the Test Tube* (Stanford: Stanford University Press, 1997), 180. My thanks to Mark Wrathall for showing me this passage.

they will, as well as that their coming to pass is not something that one can will. We must work for them, but only our continued work—and, more importantly, that of the Father—guarantees that they will come to pass. Their coming to pass is not guaranteed by the state of the world, by the given. To have faith is to trust that the Father can bring about the work that he promises to do.

Further, if we understand hope in terms of openness, then our hope for Israel, salvation, and the coming of Christ is not only a hope for future events. It is also an orientation to the world, past, present, and future. It is a way of being-oriented that reveals my finitude and, at the same time, makes my relation to those things for which I hope fully possible. Hope as a relation of openness rather than potentiality is the possibility of genuine Kierkegaardian repetition: only if events, whether past, present, or future, are open can they signify, so only if they are open can they be repeated. Hope as a relation of openness makes it possible for me to repent. It also makes it possible to repeat the deeds of faithful saints who have come before us. We, too, can make Peter's decision. We, too, can respond as did Paul and Alma. We can be witnesses that Jesus is our Messiah every bit as much as those who witnessed his resurrection and those who felt the wounds in his side, hands, and feet.

Were there space, I would further argue that to see the connection between hope, possibility, and Kierkegaardian repetition is to understand hope in terms of the infinite—in other words, always open—responsibility of a finite being. To hope is not to be responsible in some deterministic sense such that I cause events either to be or not to be, but to be responsible in the root sense: to find myself responding to them as open, as always excessive, as requiring my response and responsibility. Hope for the gathering, for salvation, and for the coming of Christ gives me my understanding of the past, present, and future, placing me as a finite being in the world with those events as things that continually come to me with significance, significance to which I must continue to respond by repetition. Given the utopian character of hope, the responsibility of repetition is inextricably entwined with the work for justice (צדק; δικαιοσύνη). In the end, hope is the hope for biblical justice.[15] In Christian terms, hope is ultimately for atonement of the past and the future that is effected in the present.

---

15. I have argued this more fully in "Philosophy and Transcendence," *Transcendence in Philosophy and Religion* (Bloomington: Indiana University Press, 2003), 70–84, which is, itself, part of a larger set of works on justice and community, in process.

A Goldilocks God:
Open Theism As a Feuerbachian Alternative?

by J. Aaron Simmons and John Sanders

I.

In contemporary philosophy of religion (and philosophical theology), abstract, indeterminate, and largely continental, discourse about God's absence is sometimes placed in stark opposition to concrete, overly determinate, and largely analytic, discourse about God's presence. In this paper we argue that this recent trend, which appears to force a decision between extremes, misses the importance of living in the space between—where one's God-talk would be characterized by epistemic humility and also theological determinacy. Somewhere between the temptations toward apophatic indeterminacy and kataphatic arrogance is where existence happens as we try to live *before* God and *with* others *in* our historical context. Drawing on Ludwig Feuerbach's rejection of positive theology as anthropocentric arrogance and negative theology as cowardice, we suggest that Open Theism productively maintains the tension between absence and presence that is required of us as *existing individuals*.[1]

II.

Though certainly well known for his critique of the arrogance that attends the positive anthropocentric and anthropomorphic claims to know God,

---

1. On this point we are implicitly drawing on Søren Kierkegaard, a thinker who also successfully walked the line between presence and absence in his philosophy of religion.

Ludwig Feuerbach also challenges negative alternatives. [2] We will briefly look at both of his criticisms as a way of setting the stage for a consideration of contemporary trends.

Feuerbach's critique of religion is well-known and in the third of his *Lectures on the Essence of Religion* he claims that "this doctrine of mine is briefly as follows":

> *Theology is anthropology*: in other words, the object of religion, which in Greek we call *theos* and in our language *God*, expresses nothing other than the essence of man; man's God is nothing other than the deified essence of man, so that the history of religion or, what amounts to the same thing, of God—for the gods are as varied as the religions, and the religions are as varied as mankind—is nothing other than the history of man.[3]

Just as the "pagan god . . . is merely an object of pagan religion," the "Christian God is merely an object of the Christian religion and consequently only a characteristic expression of the spirit and disposition of Christian man."[4] As such, neither the pagan gods nor the Christian God exists in objective reality, but is instead "a being who exists only in the faith and imagination" of the members of the specific religious community.[5] "Just like the pagan gods," Feuerbach writes, "the Christian God originated in man. If He differs from the pagan gods, it is only because Christian man is different from pagan man."[6] When understood as anthropology, theology does not tell us anything about God, but our God-talk says a lot about us. When theologians become anthropologists, Feuerbach argues that they will also find religious discourse as fundamentally arrogant insofar as particular communities universalize their local perspectives as objective truth.

According to Feuerbach, considering one's own, or one's community's, account of God to be the only plausible, or most rational, account—as some working within analytic philosophy of religion such as William Lane Craig and Richard Swinburne sometimes seem to do—is to forget the origin of religion itself: historical human existence and the natural world in which this existence is situated. In this way, Feuerbach's critique of religion, and especially of Christianity, displays both an epistemic (read anthropological) dimension in that it encourages a robust humility in light of the contingent

---

2. For an excellent consideration of Feuerbach's thought, see Van A. Harvey, *Feuerbach and the Interpretation of Religion* (Cambridge: Cambridge University Press, 1995).

3. Ludwig Feuerbach, *Lectures on the Essence of Religion*, trans. Ralph Manheim (New York: Harper and Row, 1967), 17.

4. Ibid., 17.

5. Ibid.

6. Ibid., 19.

plurality of discourses, and also a moral (read socio-political) dimension in that it encourages a patient and invitational relationship to alternative views. In contrast to the arrogance and exclusivism of determinate theology, Feuerbach understands atheism to be "positive and affirmative," such that it:

> gives back to nature and mankind the dignity of which theism has despoiled them; it restores life to nature and mankind, which theism had drained of their best powers. God, as we have seen, is jealous of nature and man; He wants man to honor, love, and serve Him alone; He wants everything else to be nothing and Himself alone to be something; in other words, theism is jealous of man and the world and begrudges them any good. Envy, ill will, and jealousy are destructive, negative passions. Atheism, on the other hand, is liberal, openhanded, open-minded; an atheist acknowledges every being's will and talent; his heart delights in the beauty of nature and the virtue of man: joy and love do not destroy, they are life-giving, affirmative.[7]

Although he was surely no friend of determinate religious belief and identity, Feuerbach was also skeptical of those "religious" gestures that would abandon such belief in favor of indeterminacy. We might say, then, that Feuerbach would be just as critical of theological liberalism as he is of classical theism. For Feuerbach, the generally negative strategy of apophatic theology is just as problematic as positive theology because it, too, turns away from "nature and man" in favor of something beyond the "concrete historical material" from which everything is drawn and to which everything refers.[8] Though Feuerbach considers all theology to be essentially anthropomorphic and something that we would do well to abandon, he is frequently critical of the way in which God-talk fails to be determinate enough to meet the real needs of the people looking for solace in religion.[9] Feuerbach claims that denying "all the qualities of a being is equivalent to denying the being himself."[10] His reason is that "a being without qualities is one which cannot become an object to the mind,

---

7. Ibid., 283.

8. Ibid., 21.

9. There is clearly a difference for Feuerbach between something's being important relative to some existential need and something's being true relative to the way things are. For example, in the twentieth of his *Lectures on the Essence of Religion*, Feuerbach claims that "religion demands of images . . . that they be useful to man, that they help him in distress; and for this reason it endows its images with life—for only living beings can help—and, specifically, human life, not only with the appearance, the outer form of life as the artist does, but also with actual life, with human feeling, human needs and passions, and even offers them food and drink (183–84).

10. Ludwig Feuerbach, *The Essence of Christianity*, trans. George Eliot (New York: Harper and Brothers Publishers, 1957), 14.

and such a being is virtually non-existent."[11] In what could be read as a direct critique of deconstructive proposals of "religion without religion" by such thinkers as Jacques Derrida and John D. Caputo,[12] Feuerbach suggests that:

> To the truly religious man, God is not a being without qualities, because to him he is a positive, real being. The theory that God cannot be defined, and consequently cannot be known by man, is therefore the offspring of recent times, a product of modern unbelief.[13]

To use Caputo's language, we might say that for Feuerbach, all "weak theologies"[14] that stress the indeterminacy of God and the translatability of all divine names into other names, are simply contemporary versions of classical atheism:

> The denial of determinate, positive predicates concerning the divine nature is nothing else than a denial of religion, with, however, an appearance of religion in its favour, so that it is not recognized as a denial; it is simply a subtle, disguised atheism. The alleged religious horror of limiting God by positive predicates is only the irreligious wish to know nothing more of God, to banish God from the mind. Dread of limitation is dread of existence.[15]

Removing all ambiguity on this front, and decidedly demonstrating the mistake it would be to consider him *only* a critic of kataphatic determinacy, Feuerbach concludes his thought on this matter by claiming that "A God who is injured by determinate qualities *has not the courage and the strength to exist.*"[16]

Though we do not find Feuerbach's own prescription for how to avoid the problems associated with religion to be of much use, namely, the recommendation that we simply abandon religion altogether and instead focus on the way anthropology can tell us about the "essence" of human existence, we do think he is exceptionally helpful for diagnosing the condition with which

---

11. Ibid.

12. John D. Caputo, *The Prayers and Tears of Jacques Derrida: Religion without Religion* (Bloomington and Indianapolis: Indiana University Press, 1997).

13. Feuerbach, *Essence of Christianity*, 14.

14. Caputo differentiates "strong theologies," which attribute a specific name to God, from "weak theologies," which recognize that all names are inadequate to the "event." "In a strong theology," Caputo writes, "the name of God has historical determinacy and specificity—it is Christian or Jewish or Islamic, for example— whereas a weak theology, weakened by the flux of undecidability and translatability, is more open-ended." John D. Caputo, *The Weakness of God: A Theology of the Event* (Bloomington and Indianapolis: Indiana University Press, 2006), 9.

15. Feuerbach, *Essence of Christianity*, 15.

16. Ibid.; emphasis added.

contemporary philosophy of religion must deal. In sum, Feuerbach illumi-
nates both the temptation to arrogance that can accompany extremes in both
positive and negative directions: arrogance and indeterminacy, respectively.

III.

Martin Luther King, Jr.'s notion of being an "extremist for justice,"
notwithstanding, it is usually a good idea to avoid extremes. As any
child will learn from the story of Goldilocks, the porridge's being too hot
or too cold is good reason to keep looking for other bowls of porridge. This
childhood lesson is something that contemporary philosophers of religion
and philosophical theologians would do well to remember. Classically, the
distinction between positive and negative theology is more a matter of the
adequacy of human discourse in relation to the divine, than it is a concern
about God's presence (or absence).[17] While certainly drawing heavily upon
these traditional disagreements, contemporary philosophy of religion has frequently shifted the debate over linguistic expression to a debate about theological ontology. In other words, traditional disputes between apophatic and
kataphatic alternatives, seem to be more about who *God* is (or is not, or may
be) and less about who *we* are as existing individuals trying to speak about
God. Discussions about the limits of language have seemingly become debates about the (im)possibility of God. Although surely the linguistic and
ontological dimensions are intimately connected (as we have learned from
Heidegger and Derrida as well as from Austin and Davidson), we think that
Feuerbach's dual critique helps us to understand that it is important not to
confuse human ability with divine reality.

Within the contemporary literature, some thinkers articulate a notion
of God that is "more radical" than other accounts because it allows God to
signify non-ontologically and beyond any historical expression or articula-
tion. However, some thinkers resist the "relativistic" and "deconstructive"
tendencies of postmodernism by remaining firm proponents of the God of
classical theism as understood internal to a framework of metaphysical real-
ism. Though these debates often get cashed out as matter of terminology and
poetics, they tend to reflect entrenched orthodoxies: both apophatic and also
kataphatic, depending on the particular tradition in which one is working.

---

17. Which is not to say that all discourse is equally inadequate; see, for example,
William Franke, ed., *On What Cannot Be Said: Apophatic Discourses in Philosophy,
Religion, Literature, and the Arts* (Notre Dame: University of Notre Dame Press, 2007).

IV.

In much of the continental tradition, it frequently seems that the goal of philosophy of religion is to push "God-talk" to its vanishing point. This sort of view can be found in the work of those thinkers who appropriate the structure of religious experience and practice, but are critical of the doxastic content accompanying such structures and the traditional formulations in which it has been articulated and expressed. In general, then, much of the God-talk in the deconstructive tradition is focused on the significance of God's absence rather than the manifestation of God's presence. Consider, for instance, Emmanuel Levinas's claim that God must be thought of as "transcendent to the point of absence,"[18] Derrida's idea of a "messianism without a messiah,"[19] and Caputo's suggestion that the "name of God" signals "something familiar, even commonplace, yet bottomless, always on the tip of our tongue yet incomprehensible."[20]

Though it might be tempting to describe continental philosophy of religion as exemplified by Levinas, Derrida, and Caputo, among others,[21] as engaging in something bearing a striking resemblance to negative theology, all of these thinkers contend that it would be wrong to understand their work in this way.[22] They do so, in part, because they worry that even though negative theology stresses the inadequacy of human language about the divine, it seems to leave the ontological categories of classical theism in place. Operat-

18. Emmanuel Levinas, *God, Death, and Time*, trans. Bettina Bergo (Stanford: Stanford University Press, 2000), 219–24.

19. Jacques Derrida, *Specters of Marx: The State of the Debt, the Work of Mourning, and the New International*, trans. Peggy Kamuf (New York: Routledge, 1994). For other texts in which Derrida offers sustained considerations of religion, John D. Caputo, ed., *Deconstruction in a Nutshell: A Conversation with Jacques Derrida* (New York: Fordham University Press, 1997), 19–28; Jacques Derrida, *Acts of Religion*, ed. Gil Anidjar (New York and London: Routledge Press, 2002); Jacques Derrida, *The Gift of Death*, trans. David Wills (Chicago and London: The University of Chicago Press, 1995); Jacques Derrida, *Circumfession: Fifty-Nine Periods and Periphrases*, in Geoffrey Bennington and Jacques Derrida, *Jacques Derrida* (Chicago: The University of Chicago Press, 1993).

20. Caputo, *Weakness of God*, 7.

21. There are many more varieties of continental philosophy of religion, but in this essay we will focus on this phenomenological trajectory occurring in the wake of Derrida. That said, the God-talk occurring in these other trajectories is still often about God's absence rather than God's presence, albeit in a number of different ways. See, for example the work of Slavoj Žižek, Gianni Vattimo, Alain Badiou, and Giles Deleuze.

22. See, Levinas, *God, Death and Time*, 138; Jacques Derrida, "Différance," in *Margins of Philosophy*, trans. Alan Bass (Chicago: University of Chicago Press, 1985), 1–28. See also, Howard Coward and Toby Foshay, eds., *Derrida and Negative Theology* (Albany: State University of New York Press, 1992).

ing in a phenomenological trajectory, these continental philosophers of religion attempt to relocate the focus of God-talk from the nature of the divine to the way in which such God-talk operates in human discourse and social praxis. Accordingly, one might worry that there is just not much *God* in this God-talk, at least not insofar as "God" has been traditionally understood by the majority of the proponents of the world's religions.[23] For ease of reference, we will label this general perspective as a *theology of absence*.[24]

As a way of making sense of the theology of absence as found in deconstructive "religion without religion," consider Caputo's definitions of 'deconstruction' and 'religion':

> Deconstruction is a passion and a prayer for the impossible, a defense of the impossible against its critics, a plea for/to the experience of the impossible, which is the only real experience, stirring with religious passion. By religion I mean a pact with the impossible, a covenant with the unrepresentable, a promise made by the *tout autre* with its people, where we are all the people of the *tout autre*, the people of the promise, promised over to the promise.[25]

Here we can see the structural appropriation of religious terminology without a commitment to any determinate religious tradition.[26] The "God" of a theology of absence is the "*tout autre*" (i.e., the *absolutely other*) not Jesus, Allah, or Yahweh, for such names are already too determinate, too constrained, and too final. Accordingly, deconstructive religion is presented as a religion of the "without" (*sans*) rather than of the "with." "Deconstruction regularly," Caputo says,

---

23. For a good consideration of the relation of positive and negative theology, see Jean-Luc Marion, *The Visible and the Revealed*, trans. Christina M. Gschwandtner, et al. (New York: Fordham University Press, 2008), chapter 6.

24. One might term this a "metaphysics of absence," but given the complicated relationship between continental philosophy and the idea of metaphysics, we have chosen to use "theology," here. As an example of this complicated relationship, see Levinas who explicitly advocates a return to "metaphysics," but in so doing he redefines it not as a speculative and systematic philosophical enterprise, but as the desire for the invisible. See, Emmanuel Levinas, *Totality and Infinity: An Essay on Exteriority*, trans. Alphonso Lingis (Pittsburgh: Duquesne University Press, 1969), section I, A. See also, Edith Wyschogrod, *Emmanuel Levinas: The Problem of Ethical Metaphysics* (New York: Fordham University Press, 2000); and Adriaan Theodoor Peperzak, *Beyond: The Philosophy of Emmanuel Levinas* (Evanston: Northwestern University Press, 1997), 231–33.

25. Caputo, *Prayers and Tears*, xx.

26. And *perhaps* with the rejection of all such traditions, but we will leave this issue aside here.

rhythmically repeats this religiousness, *sans* the concrete, historical religions; it repeats nondogmatically the religious structure of experience, the category of the religious. It repeats the passion for the messianic promise and messianic expectation, *sans* the concrete messianisms of the positive religions that wage endless war and spill the blood of the other, and that, anointing themselves God's chosen people, are consummately dangerous to everyone else who is not so chosen; . . . . it repeats the movements of faith, of expecting what we cannot know but only believe . . . of the blindness of faith *sans savoir, sans avoir, sans voir* . . . in the impossible, but without the dogmas of the positive religious faiths.[27]

Without knowing, *without* having, *without* seeing. In the theology of absence, "God" is no longer an existing being in a distinct relation to the world, but a name that we humans give to an experience of (a relation to and a way of life in response to) the absolutely other. The "*sans*" is meant to allow for alterity to signify as such and, accordingly, a theology of absence is stringently opposed to what has been termed "onto-theo-logy." Following Heidegger, we might say that "God" should be heard as an inadequate attempt to relate to an event that can't be adequately understood, and not as a proper name describing the highest being.[28]

Though there are substantive, and often legitimate, replies that could be offered by defenders of deconstructive approaches to God-talk regarding the ethical problems of ontology (Levinas), the limits and interruptions of human discourse (Derrida), and the tendencies toward violence of strong theologies (Caputo), the core of Feuerbach's challenge to negative strategies remains in place: in quite sensibly and admirably trying to preserve the transcendence, the alterity, the distance, the holiness of what we name "God", we come close to making a hash out of God-talk altogether because it can seem to disconnect such talk from the living traditions in which it has been given shape. For Feuerbach, the appropriation of religious structure without determinate content amounts to practical atheism. B. Keith Putt suggests something similar in his critique of Caputo's weak theology of the event: "In so assiduously avoiding connecting God with Being or with Super-Essential

---

27. Caputo, *Prayers and Tears*, xxi.

28. See Heidegger, "The Onto-theo-logical Constitution of Metaphysics" and "Philosophy and Theology," both included in John D. Caputo, ed., *The Religious* (Oxford: Blackwell, 2002); and "Nietzsche's Word: God is Dead," in Martin Heidegger, *The Question Concerning Technology and Other Essays*, trans. William Lovitt (New York: Harper and Row, 1977), 53–112. For more on Heidegger's relation to Christian theology see, John Macquarrie, *Heidegger and Christianity* (New York: Continuum Press, 1994); John D. Caputo, *The Mystical Element in Heidegger's Thought* (New York: Fordham University Press, 1978).

Personhood, Caputo may well undermine his own poetics of a loving, suf-fering God of justice by positing a God functionally indistinguishable from Aristotle's *nous noetikos*."[29] Moving further in this direction, Kevin Hart even suggests that Caputo comes close to deploying something like a theologically modernist account of religious pluralism:

> The only religion one can plausibly endorse is one that is not committed to an exclusive religion. Once again, we see the Enlightenment model: religion is a genus of which the positive religions are the species. And once again we can see how "religion without religion" follows the En-lightenment program of passing from the positive religions to a universal religiosity that has remained pure because it has always abided in the realm of possibility.[30]

Accordingly, the distance that emerges in such passages between Feuer-bach and the defenders of "religion without religion" might plausibly be cashed out in at least two ways. On the one hand, it could be claimed that Feuerbach's naturalism is more uncompromising and, on the other hand, it could be claimed that his abandonment of God-talk is more consistent. While Derrida and Caputo, say, are quite resistant to the "supernatural," as it were, they are not naturalists in the way that Feuerbach is. Surely the impos-sibility of justice, the event, the call of the other, etc., are all not necessarily reducible to what might be termed "natural" phenomena. Moreover, though Derrida and Caputo share Feuerbach's frustration with the possible arrogance and violence that can accompany determinate theisms, they remain willing to deploy God-talk as something that contributes to a better world.[31]

V.

In contrast to the broadly negative trajectory of deconstructive philosophy of religion, in the more mainstream, and generally more analytic, approach, the goal appears to be the maintenance of a particular account of (usually, *specifically*) Christian orthodoxy (whether affirmatively as in "Christian phi-losophy" or negatively as in the prominent atheistic voices challenging such

---

29. B. Keith Putt, "Risking Love and the Divine "Perhaps": Postmodern Poetics of a Vulnerable God," *Perspectives in Religious Studies* 34, no.2 (Summer 2007): 193–214, 205.

30. Kevin Hart, "Without," in Zlomislić and DeRoo, eds., *Cross and Khôra: Deconstruction and Christianity in the Work of John D. Caputo* (Eugene, Ore.: Pickwick Publications, 2010), 80–108, 95.

31. We are content to leave it as an open question whether this willingness signifies an improvement over Feuerbach's account, or a failure to own up to the implications of their own premises.

notions). According to this approach one should speak of God rather than "God"—that is, the real divine life is the object of inquiry and not merely a word in a natural language, or some impossible event that detaches theo-poetics from ontological status. This perspective is perhaps best represented by those philosophers of religion who engage in classically oriented "apologetic" enterprises,[32] especially in an offensive mode and not merely a defensive one, e.g., consider Richard Swinburne and William Lane Craig. Since this philosophical trajectory is one that attempts to give rational proofs of the truth of determinate religious beliefs concerning God's existence and divine nature, we will refer to this perspective as a *theology of presence.*[33]

Even within the theology of presence, very few philosophers still think that the existence of God can be deductively demonstrated. Nonetheless, many contend that the belief in the existence of God can be given strong inductive support. For example, Craig explicitly claims that certainty is not available in rational argumentation regarding Christianity:

> Now some Christian believers might be troubled by the notion that one's apologetic case for Christianity yields only probability rather than certainty. But the fact that Christianity can only be shown to be probably true need not be troubling. . . . To demand logically demonstrative proofs as a pre-condition for making a religious commitment is . . . just being unreasonable.[34]

Nonetheless, even stressing the broadly inductive approach to Christian apologetics before going into the various arguments for God's existence and nature that could be supplied, Craig ultimately concludes: "Hence, amazing as it may seem, the most plausible answer to the question of why something exists rather than nothing is that God exists."[35] While this is definitely a plausible answer, and maybe even the most plausible considering the range of pos-

---

32. This is not to say that all "apologetics" are problematic in similar ways. For conceptions of postmodern apologetics, see J. Aaron Simmons, "Apologetics After Objectivity," in *Reexamining Deconstruction and Determinate Religion: Toward a Religion with Religion* (Pittsburgh: Duquesne University Press, 2012); and Christina M. Gschwandtner, *Postmodern Apologetics? Arguments for God in Contemporary Philosophy* (New York and Oxford: Oxford University Press, 2012).

33. This phrase might be productively considered in relation to Derrida's notion of the "metaphysics of presence." Of course, for Derrida, the metaphysics of presence is meant to address far more than an issue in the philosophy of religion, but instead the very way of conceptualizing the world internal to linguistic structures. Nonetheless, for Derrida logocentrism and ontotheology are not unconnected.

34. William Lane Craig, *Reasonable Faith: Christian Truth and Apologetics* (Wheaton, Ill.: Crossway Books, 1994), 40.

35. Ibid., 121–22.

sibilities accepted by a particular community of discourse, how is one to understand Craig other than as saying that if one, therefore, denies the existence of God then that person is irrational insofar as s/he chooses to believe without a concern for the logical plausibility of the arguments for God? In this case, the nonbeliever might have true belief, but without proper warrant and so, would remain irrational. Even though warning that requiring explicit arguments for religious belief would "consign most believers to irrationality,"[36] Craig eventually seems to suggest that all atheists would be irrational, given the weight of the arguments for God's existence.

We are not saying that Craig *does* suggest this, but the fact that it is plausible to read him in this way remains problematic given the lived contexts in which humans engage in philosophical speculation and theological reflection. In this sense, Feuerbach might claim that Craig does not attend carefully enough to his own historical location within a particular tradition. Indeed, Craig himself recognizes significant limits to philosophical discourse in the final chapter of *Reasonable Faith* when he claims that the "ultimate apologetic involves two relationships: your relationship with God and your relationships with others."[37] Stressing the lived dimension of human existence, one might think that Craig would be more receptive to theories of truth that do not reduce to the relationship of a proposition to a state of affairs, but instead allows for what Caputo might term an "eventful" or "narratival" dimension within a Feuerbachian anthropological appreciation of the dynamic plurality of contexts.

In light of the distinctions between the theology of absence and the theology of presence, we want to stress that drawing such lines between these two perspectives does not mean that *all* continental philosophy or *all* analytic philosophy divides so neatly. The space between these two extremes of absence and presence, is inhabited by *both* continental philosophers *and also* analytic philosophers [i.e., there are many theologically determinate continental philosophers of religion (e.g., Merold Westphal, Bruce Ellis Benson, and James K.A. Smith) and many epistemically humble analytic philosophers of religion (e.g., Nicholas Wolterstorff, William Hasker, and C. Stephen Evans)]. While it is important to avoid compromise just for the sake of compromise, we believe that the theology of absence and the theology of presence are rightly understood as extremes that should be resisted rather than as exclusive options between which we must choose. Our suggestion is that the questions,

---

36. Ibid., 37.

37. Ibid., 299. See also the person relative accounts of justification, e.g., George Mavrodes, *Belief in God: A Study in the Epistemology of Religion* (New York: Random House, 1970), chap. 2. See also, Michael Polyani, *Personal Knowledge: Towards a Post-Critical Philosophy* (Chicago: University of Chicago Press, 1974).

"Either presence or absence?" and "Either continental philosophy or analytic philosophy?" are much too stark of dichotomies to be of significant use in *lived* religious existence and productive philosophical inquiry. As such, we hope that thinking between such extremes will open spaces for not only a more theologically sustainable perspective (given the contextual realities of human existence), but also a more philosophically promising practice that will continue to erode the impermeable wall that is sometimes understood to stand between analytic and continental approaches.

VI.

Importantly, it is not immediately clear what would lie in the middle of these extremes of presence and absence. In order to take seriously this in-between, as it were, it is crucial that we not simply try to overcome these extremes by quickly rejecting them outright. Resistance need not mean dismissal or disregard. We can only productively resist these extremes (and open a space for standing between them) by taking them both seriously as each getting certain things quite right. Namely, the theology of absence correctly understands the importance of emphasizing the contingency and contextualism of all human discourse and the importance of viewing religious belief and practice as a risky investment made by existing individuals. This contextual reality of all religious existence is something such existential thinkers as Kierkegaard, Dostoevsky, and Heidegger all understood quite well. Importantly, there are both epistemic and ontological components to such contextualism. These dual aspects can be seen in Caputo's resistance to "strong theology." As Putt convincingly argues, Caputo agrees with Jean-Luc Marion that "onto-centric language [of classical theism] often tempts individuals toward committing 'conceptual idolatry,' specifically the idolatry of power, prestige, and absolute knowledge."[38] Instead of a God of self-sufficiency, the theology of absence talks about a God who vulnerably loves. "Along with the risk inherent in love itself," Putt claims, "Caputo also recognizes an epistemic risk that remains within the structure of his weak theology."[39] Divine vulnerability and epistemic humility are, thus, key components of this perspective. These "postmodern" aspects, should not be abandoned in a move to the middle, but should be appropriated in such a way that God-talk does not reduce to an arrogant (and, hence, self-forgetting) anthropomorphic anthropocentrism.

---

38. Putt, "Risking Love," 198. The passage from Marion quoted by Caputo is from Jean-Luc Marion, *God Without Being: Hors-Texte*, trans. Thomas A. Carlson (Chicago: The University of Chicago Press, 1991), 16–17.

39. Putt, "Risking Love," 196.

Moving in the opposite direction, the theology of presence correctly understands the importance of standing within historical traditions of determinate religious belief and practice. From this perspective, talk of a deconstructive "religion *without* religion"[40] can miss something crucial about human existence precisely because of the role that local narratives play in the stories in which we find ourselves. Indeed, forgetting such location can lead to the arrogance that their positions are ostensibly constructed to avoid. The task that confronts contemporary continental philosophy of religion, and Caputo himself admits this, is to remember that "religion without religion" can itself quickly become another determinate tradition alongside a *postmodern Christianity*, a *postmodern Islam*, or a *postmodern Hinduism*, for example.[41] Moreover, the theology of presence allows for our discourse potentially to get some things right about God and expresses this possibility in its concern for logical argument, entailments of accepted premises, adequacy to historical theology, and perhaps even in its attention to ecclesial and scriptural authorities. Importantly, though it might appear that the theology of presence *tends toward* certainty and *seems to assume* universal assent from rational persons, in no way does this assume epistemic infallibilism. But, it is one thing to say that "of course we could be wrong about X" and another thing to make this integral to the way one engages in philosophical inquiry.

In summary, then, while the theology of absence rightly stresses the importance of attending to God's distance (as expressed by the *"sans"* and the *"tout autre"*), the theology of presence rightly stresses the importance of attending to God's proximity (as revealed in the incarnation, scripture, and revelation, say). We contend that we must take both of these trajectories seriously while also recognizing that they can both give rise to problematic extremes on a spectrum of possible options.

Our suggestion is that we need some sort of *Postmodern Kataphaticism*[42] that would understand these two extremes as *temptations* to which we are al-

---

40. Caputo, *The Prayers and Tears of Jacques Derrida.*

41. Importantly, Caputo and Derrida are both very cognizant of this issue, though they tend to approach it as something to be wary of rather than something to embrace. See, J. Aaron Simmons, "Continuing to Look for *God in France*: On the Relationship Between Phenomenology and Theology," in *Words of Life: New Theological Turns in French Phenomenology*, ed. Bruce Ellis Benson and Norman Wirzba (New York: Fordham University Press, 2010), 15–29.

42. See J. Aaron Simmons, "Postmodern Kataphaticism? A Constructive Proposal," *Analecta Hermeneutica* 4 (2012), in a special issue edited by Michelle Rebidoux entitled, "Refiguring Divinity: Continental Philosophy of Religion." Available online at: http://journals.library.mun.ca/ojs/index.php/analecta/article/view/709/609 (accessed April 12, 2016).

ways drawn and of which we must constantly be cautious. However, it is by recognizing these extremes *as tempting* that we can see why the productive space between these two perspectives insists upon a constant tension between the extremes themselves and not a final choice of one *over* the other. When we begin to slide too far toward anthropocentric arrogance (whether expressed as an epistemological or theological claim) we must be pulled back toward the inescapability of our existential location in-a-world (as both Martin Heidegger and Nicholas Wolterstorff would say). When we begin to slide too far toward a notion of God-talk that requires us to abandon the tradition we are attempting to deconstructively rethink, then we must be pulled back toward the historical commitments regarding the specificity of the divine life that have defined the tradition itself. *A deconstructive, and yet orthodox, approach need not be seen as a contradictory notion, even if it should be seen as a risky one.* Postmodern Kataphaticism can *legitimately* be postmodern and *legitimately* be kataphatic. Some risks are well worth taking and we think that this is one such risk.[43]

It is important to realize that the two extremes that we are discussing do not simply stand as endpoints on an easily continuous line.[44] Though the two perspectives differ on what notions of God remain philosophically and theologically viable, they do so by focusing on different dimensions of religious existence. Accordingly, modeling the space between the two extremes requires a bit more complicated structure than simply a line with two discrete end-points. We propose the following: A four-quadrant grid where the x-axis tracks ontological determinacy and the y-axis tracks epistemological humility. On this grid, the theology of absence will score high on the y-axis and low on the x-axis, while the theology of presence will likely score high on the x-axis and low on the y-axis.[45] As such, if the theology of absence gets placed in the upper left quadrant and the theology of presence gets placed in the lower right quadrant, then there is a diagonal line that can be drawn connecting the two points such that they are in a direct relationship (see chart).

---

43. James K.A. Smith claims that there is often nothing more heterodox in continental philosophy of religion as orthodoxy. James K.A. Smith, "Continental Philosophy of Religion: Prescriptions for a Healthy Subdiscipline," *Faith and Philosophy* 26, no.4 (October 2009): 440–48. In his more positive moments, which should definitely be read together with his more negative gestures, John Caputo can be read as saying something similar. See, for example, John D Caputo, *What Would Jesus Deconstruct? The Good News of Postmodernism for the Church* (Grand Rapids: Baker Books, 2007); *Philosophy and Theology* (Nashville: Abingdon Press, 2006).

44. We are grateful to William Abraham for helping us to work out this point.

45. Of course, many proponents of religion without religion seem pretty certain of their perspective.

```
                          Humility
                            |
                            |
  Theologies of Absence     |   Open Theism and other
                            |           views
                            |
Indeterminate  ─────────────┼───────────────────── Determinate
                            |
                            |
                            |   Theologies of Presence
                            |
                            |
                        Arrogance
```

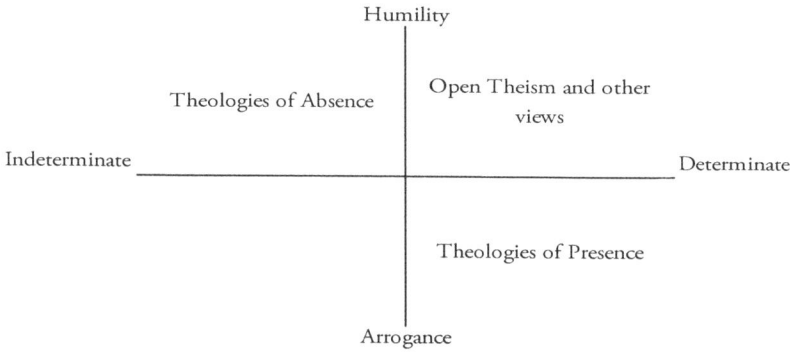

However, given the range of options in the philosophy of religion and the variety of approaches one might take to such options, we propose that the goal is not to move to the center of this line, but to move toward the upper-right quadrant so far as possible, which is defined by both ontological (and historical) determinacy and also epistemic humility. Interestingly, both of these components are a result of one's context, we believe. In such a move, there are likely new lines that will be drawn such that the relation of the alternatives to the extremes is slightly different in each case. When plotted this way, the two accounts are legitimately understood as tempting extremes relative to which a middle-ground could be found (albeit when understood in a radial way)—a middle-ground that is both existentially aware (and, hence, epistemically humble) and also theologically determinate (and, hence, historically, traditionally, and liturgically attentive).

VII.

Although there is surely a wide variety of alternatives that would appropriately occupy a middle-ground between theologies of absence and theologies of presence, we will look at one model in particular as especially promising: Open theism as propounded by such thinkers as William Hasker, Clark Pinnock, and Dean Zimmerman, among others.[46] The openness model of God was developed by analytic philosophers of religion and theologians situated in the evangelical tradition. The piety and particularly the prayer life of evangelical Christians require a deity who cares about and responds to the prayers and tears of people. Evangelical theologians and philosophers are definitely on the side of theologies of presence since their God has definite

---

46. There are other analytic philosophers of religion, Nicholas Wolterstorff, for example, who have defended dynamic omniscience (which will be discussed below), but have stopped short of explicitly identifying themselves as open theists.

properties. In addition, they are confident they "know" what God is like via biblical and philosophical claims. Unfortunately, though, it is common for evangelical philosophers and theologians to sound exceedingly confident about their philosophical arguments and the virtual certainty of their theological positions. As Nancey Murphy has argued, this is because evangelicals have largely accepted the Enlightenment project of strong foundationalism, language as referential, and a stringent version of evidentialism.[47]

Despite such problematic excesses within evangelical theology, open theism arises out of the evangelical tradition and understands itself as part of a determinate religious community. Consequently, open theists affirm that God possesses determinate characteristics and so definitely has the courage and strength to exist. Yet, proponents of the openness of God have, from the start, emphasized a commitment to epistemic and theological humility. In the book, *The Openness of God*, the authors state in the preface that "We do not claim that the open view is the only model with biblical or philosophical support. . . .We know that our arguments are open to question, and we welcome the discussion we hope they will generate."[48] The authors rejected the strong foundationalism and quest for epistemic certainty endemic to much evangelical thought. Pinnock, for example, pointed to a key change in thinking when he finally became aware that theologians are "fallible and historically situated creatures" and, importantly, he actually applied these ideas to himself and began to see how much he needed to learn from others.[49] He says he changed from possessing a "fortress mentality" to one of going on a "theological pilgrimage." Open theist philosopher David Basinger says "while I do not doubt there is objective religious truth . . . the way I conceptualize such truth is simply one way in which this truth can be understood."[50] There seems to be an inherent call for humility in open theism given its determinate understanding of God as one who listens to creaturely input and often makes decisions based upon it.

---

47. Nancey Murphy, *Beyond Liberalism and Fundamentalism: How Modern and Postmodern Philosophy Set the Theological Agenda* (Valley Forge, Pa.: Trinity Press International, 1996).

48. Clark Pinnock, Richard Rice, John Sanders, William Hasker, and David Basinger, *The Openness of God: a Biblical Challenge to the Traditional Understanding of God* (Downers Grove, Ill.: InterVarsity Press, 1994), 9–10.

49. Pinnock, "From Augustine to Arminius: A Pilgrimage in Theology" in Pinnock, ed., *The Grace of God, The Will of Man* (Grand Rapids, Mich.: Zondervan, 1989), 16. It is common for evangelical theologians to say they are finite and potentially fallible but they rarely apply this to their own theologizing.

50. Basinger, "Religious Belief Formation: A Kantian Perspective Informed by Science," in *God in an Open Universe: Science, Metaphysics, and Open Theism*, ed. William Hasker, Thomas Jay Oord, and Dean Zimmerman (Eugene, Ore.: Pickwick, 2011), 66.

Hence, proponents of open theism combine epistemic humility with historically determinate religious beliefs and practices. Their communities have shaped the forms of piety as well as biblical notions to which they appeal in making their case for the openness of God. What we find to be especially promising about open theism is that it inhabits the in-between of the extremes of presence and absence in a way that illustrates the importance of one's contextual location and personal history when considering how to respond to the particular temptation with which one is faced. For example, some open theists might be more seduced by the temptation toward an epistemic extreme of over-confidence (we should remember that Richard Swinburne is an open theist) while other open theists might be more seduced by the temptation toward a theological extreme of indeterminacy.

A key motivation for the development of open theism was the recognition of an incongruity between particular forms of evangelical piety and the classical theist model of God propounded by many evangelical thinkers. A God responsive to prayer is taken for granted in evangelical piety but the God of classical theism is strongly immutable and impassible such that it is logically impossible for God to respond to creatures. Open theists have reformed some of these ideas in order to help people live as Christians, to offer a better explanation of the biblical portrayal of God, and to be more theologically and philosophically coherent. Open theists emphasize that God is open to what creatures do and that the future is open in that there is more than one possible future (like a create your own story book). God enters into genuine give-and-receive relations with creatures. God responds to contingencies and adjusts divine plans, if necessary, to take into account the decisions of free creatures. God employs flexible strategies when working with creatures. The divine-human interaction is more like playing jazz together than algorithmically following a blueprint. Though the divine love and faithfulness remain constant, God is affected by what creatures do and the divine life experiences changes as God interacts in various relationships. Also, due to creaturely freedom, it is possible for them to thwart particular divine aspirations and bring about evil states of affairs. Since God is affected by what creatures do, open theists claim that even God has a history.

For open theists this implies that there is no fixed blueprint for the future. The future is not set in stone so God knows what we call "the" future not as a finished necessity, but as a host of possibilities. Open theists affirm that God possesses "dynamic omniscience" according to which God has exhaustive knowledge of the past and present and knows the future as possibilities and probabilities.[51] Even the exact nature of the *eschaton* is not settled because it depends not only upon God but also upon what creatures do. If God employs flexible strategies and utilizes multiple routes in the attempt to achieve divine ends then we need to be circumspect about our assurance of the Spirit's leading. The biblical writers depict quite a few episodes in which the people of God were surprised at the direction God had taken. Nobody, for instance, anticipated the inclusion of the Gentiles into the people of God apart from Sabbath observance, dietary regulations, and male circumcision. Acts 15 records the contentious debate about this issue in the early Christian community. Through prayer and dialogue most of the early Jewish Christians concluded that God wanted to include Gentiles into the people of God without requiring them to convert to Judaism first. They decided that this was the direction of the Holy Spirit. This was a turning point in the history of the Jesus movement but not all Jewish followers of Jesus accepted this conclusion. The New Testament evidences a number of debates about Christian practices (e.g., marriage, festivals, foods, etc.), and it is clear from the texts that the early Christian community did not always agree on the leading of the Spirit. One reason for this is that divine guidance is not over powering which means that God takes risks by relying on humans.

However, for open theists, religious disagreement may not always be due to our failure to listen to God. For many aspects of life God does not have a blueprint for us to follow, rather, God is interested what we want to do. On many occasions the divine chef does not have a recipe for our lives but, instead, works with us as we create a recipe. God is open to the great diversity among human cultures as well as between individuals so we should not be surprised that God is pleased with a fair amount of diversity in worship and theology. This does not mean that God approves of everything we do since we can be quite creative when it comes to evil. But in matters that are not evil God may not always have a particular preference. By metaphorically describing the Christian community as engaged in playing jazz with God, we are able to say that it is likely that, just as in an improvisational jam-session, the person taking the lead will shift throughout the session. So, we might say that God sometimes takes the lead and we will fill in the background notes and at other times God expects us to lead while God takes delight in what we develop (at least for some of our activities). According to open theism, uniformity in religious belief and practice should not be expected nor desired.

---

51. John Sanders coined the term dynamic omniscience. See his *The God Who Risks: A Theology of Divine Providence*, rev. (Downers Grove, Ill.: InterVarsity Press, 2007), 15, 206–9.

Though God likely wants us to agree on some important practices, values, and beliefs it will always be the case that the gospel must be indigenized in the lives of groups and individuals. This is a theological point that yields ethical, political, and epistemic results: if God is vulnerable and open to our input we should be vulnerable and open to what others have to say.[52]

Another reason for dialogical and epistemic humility is that the theological and philosophical proponents of open theism reject strong foundationalism and the idea that there is a universal rationality, neutrally oriented and externally located beyond all social communities. They affirm that our interpretations of biblical passages do not arrive at finality and that even perfect being theology depends upon differing notions of perfection which arise out of the values of particular communities. Our theological formulations are finite, grounded in particular discourses of faith, such that our understanding is always partial and not the final word.

Given that open theists affirm that God is open to the input of creatures, that our theological reflections are finite and fallible, and that all theological proposals arise out of determinate religious communities, epistemic humility with its requisite hermeneutic charity to the input of others is entailed in this theological model. On the other hand, because of the particular Christian community out of which open theism arises, open theists are also going to affirm determinate religious beliefs and practices. Open theists agree with Feuerbach that for Christians God is a personal agent not a cipher. Proponents of openness are worried that the "God" of many of the deconstructionists has been eviscerated of any meaning and thus renders a reciprocal relationship with God impossible—with Heidegger's critique of onto-theology in mind, we should realize that one cannot sing songs to or dance with *Khora* any more readily than one sings to and dances with *Causa Sui*. Open theists think that what is offered in place of a personal God cannot nourish a religious life and they fear that the Derridean conception of God as impossible event may be nothing more than Feuerbach's "subtle, disguised atheism." The absence of God, for open theists, is framed in the biblical sense of the human cry for divine help when worshippers call on God ("How long will you hide your face from me?" (Ps. 13:1) not in the deconstructionist sense that there is no being (an entity) upon whom one may call.[53] "In him we live and move and have our being," said the Apostle Paul (Acts 17:28). It is a personal agent who calls us to participate in the divine narrative whom we worship and sing

---

52. It is surely possible that an open theist could be epistemically arrogant about the claim that God is open, but to do so is to risk inconsistency internal to the open perspective itself.

53. See the discussion of the absence and presence of God in Sanders, *The God Who Risks*, 68–70.

to and invoke for assistance, not *Khora*, the indeterminate realm of pure potentiality which cannot be directly invoked and is seemingly oblivious to our songs because it lacks personhood.

Open theists affirm that God has determinate characteristics and believe that those attributes are best disclosed in the life of Jesus. This may strike some as sliding right back into a Feuerbachian trap of anthropocentric and exclusivist arrogance but the claim is that this is the way that open theists, in their finitude, understand reality, not that this is the *only* rational way for humans to understand reality. They believe that there is a God and that they know something about the lead player of their jazz band; even if this knowledge is dependent upon finite formulations of particular religious communities and is potentially fallible. For open theists, God has the courage and strength to allow their names to accompany God's own on the marquee. To change metaphors and return to Goldilocks, open theists maintain that the porridge is not too hot (they do not know with certainty) nor is it too cold (they are not simply negative). It may not be "just right" but it is warm and edible enough to be both inviting to the hungry and nourishing to the weak.

VIII.

Open theism allows for productively moving forward in contemporary philosophy of religion and philosophical theology as embodied, historical, finite, existing individuals-in-community without requiring that we finally decide in favor of absence over presence, or vice-versa. Even though open theism, as a whole, might likely err more on the side of presence than on the side of absence, it attempts to stress the distance *and* proximity of God. For open theists, God can be rightly described as "*tout autre*" and also the loving savior of the world; affirming the one need not eliminate the possibility of affirming the other. Since human existence requires standing between the temptations to theological extremes, we should not expect the practice of philosophy of religion to be any different. While our discourse about God is unlikely to turn out to ever be "just right," as was Golidlocks' third bowl of porridge, we should still seek to provide a Postmodern Kataphatic discourse about a *Goldilocks God*— one that lies between extremes and yet in the midst of existential tension. Open theism is an approach that helps us to do just that, though, again, it is surely not the *only* one. Importantly, though, some themes are likely to be displayed in all such approaches: the importance of divine and human risk, the stress on love instead of power, the emphasis on interaction and relationship rather than self-sufficiency, and the intimacy between theology and justice. Indeed, Putt suggests that open theism and the "theopassionism" of Caputo may have quite a bit more in common than is often recognized (by either Caputo or open theists). The "emphasis upon love and vulnerability," Putt suggests, "associates

Caputo directly with open theists, such as Richard Rice, John Sanders, and Clark Pinnock, all of whom adopt a similar position [to Caputo] relative to the centrality of divine love and risk."[54]

While there is substantial work yet to be done exploring such possible connections and expanding on the ways in which these alternative traditions might be viewed as resources for each other, minimally we hope that this essay has outlined possible temptations of which philosophers of religion should be aware and in light of which they should work. We want to stress, again, that we are not accusing any particular thinkers of having actually given in to either of the two extremes of absence or presence, though it is likely that some have. However, even if we are entirely mistaken to suggest that, in general, analytic philosophy of religion is tempted by the excesses of presence and continental philosophy of religion is tempted by the excesses of absence, the fact that such *mis*interpretations are not entirely closed off by the thinkers working in the different traditions should invite us all to be more attentive to how our work is being received by interlocutors in alternative philosophical communities. The burden for the continentalists is to be more forthcoming about the metaphysical, ontological, or ethical claims operative in their work (we view such continental philosophers of religion as Merold Westphal, Richard Kearney, and Kevin Hart as examples of how to do this). The burden for the analytic philosophers is to be more responsive to the perception of hyper-rationalism and a lack of existential awareness (as examples for how to do this, we suggest such thinkers as Nicholas Wolterstorff and Clark Pinnock). Stereotypes are always dangerous, but they are also invitations to think critically about how to avoid such misunderstandings in the future.

---

54. Putt, "Risking Love," 196. Resonate with our argument here, Putt suggests that open theism might have closer ties to the work of Richard Kearney who allows a closer connection between theological discourse and philosophical ontology than does Caputo. In the vocabulary of the present essay, this suggestion might be understood to indicate that those postmodern philosophers who remain open to determinate religious beliefs and practices regarding the divine and positive religious traditions (i.e., epistemological postmodernists) are likely to be more compatible with theological perspectives that claim risk and love to describe God's relation to the world and not merely a poetics of human discourse in relation to an unnamable non-ontological alterity (i.e., metaphysical postmodernists).

A Critique of the Openness Case
for Creation *ex Nihilo*

by David Paulsen and Spencer Noorlander

In many ways, open, process, and Mormon theologians are allies against what they see as an errant mainstream theological tradition.[1] All defend libertarian freedom and agree that many of the divine attributes[2] in the conventional conception of God should be modified or rejected. Indeed, their theologies are similar enough that critics sometimes attack one by implying it ultimately leads to the other. For example, in a review of Clark Pinnock's *Most Moved Mover*, one evangelical scholar wrote, "If the[se] nascent ideas on divine corporeality . . . are any indication, it seems that the 'mature' vision of God in open theology will be more like that of Mormonism than orthodoxy."[3] Like-

---

1. See, for example, Clark Pinnock, "Overcoming a Pagan Inheritance" in *Most Moved Mover: A Theology of God's Openness* (Grand Rapids: Baker Book House, 2001), 65–111. Open theists, as well as Mormon and process thinkers, reject the following mainstream characterizations of God: all-controlling, all-determining, absolutely simple, timeless, immutable, impassible, pure actuality.

2. We follow the biblical and traditional Christian usage in using masculine pronouns to refer to God. While Mormons do affirm that God, like Christ, is an exalted man, we recognize that process and open theologians do not assign a specific gender to God. For the sake of convenience, however, we refer to God using masculine pronouns when discussing all three views, as both process and open theologians have done in their published works.

3. Jeff Riddle, "Book Review: Most Moved Mover: A Theology of God's Openness, by Clark Pinnock." Jefferson Park Baptist Church, October 15, 2003, http://www.jpbc.org/writings/br-most_moved_mover.html. Riddle's reason for seeing open theism as closer to Mormonism than orthodoxy is Pinnock's very positive exploration of the

wise, open theists face the charge of being process theists in sheep's clothing.[4]

Of course, the differences between these theologies are as significant as their similarities. Mormon and process theologians deny creation *ex nihilo* while most open theists defend it.[5] Perhaps open theists fall behind this traditional model to defend themselves against the accusation of being old process wine in new evangelical bottles.[6] We will critique the openness case for creation *ex nihilo* with the hope that doing so will lead to fruitful discourse.[7]

---

doctrine of divine embodiment. Riddle refers to this as "among the most disturbing avenues" that Pinnock explores. Riddle concludes his review by saying that open theism "diminishes rather than enhances the conception of the glory of God" (88). Also cited in Gannon Murphy, *Consuming Glory: A Classical Defense of Divine-Human Relationality Against Open Theism* (Wipf and Stock Publishers, 2006). In a review of *Most Moved Mover*, professor Christopher A. Hall similarly expresses concern that "We are only a few steps away, it seems, from the assertion that God possesses a body of sorts, spiritual though it may be." Christopher Hall, "Openness Season," *Christianity Today* 47, no. 2 (February 2003): 92.

4. See Scott Hozee, "The Openness of God," *Calvin Theological Journal* (November 1995): 589–93.

5. Not all Open theists defend creation *ex nihilo*. Thomas Oord, for example, advocates a kind of "cyclic universe . . . in which each successive universe both retains metaphysical similarities with past universes and also emerge (as created by God) as genuinely novel creations." Brint Montgomery, Thomas Oord, and Karen Winslow, eds., "Relational Love," *Relational Theology: A Contemporary Introduction* (Oregon: Wipf & Stock Pub , 2012), 36.

6. We do not claim that openness responses are acrimonious, only that open theists stand in the position of having to defend themselves against both the theological right and theological left. Since the most common critique of openness theology from the right is that it suffers the same flaws as process theology, the frequency of their defense is understandable. For openness critiques of process theology, see David Basinger, *Divine Power in Process Theism: A Philosophical Critique* (Albany: State University of New York Press, 1988); David Pinnock, et al, *The Openness of God: A Biblical Challenge to the Traditional Understanding of God* (Downers Grove, Ill.: IVP Academic, 1994), 112, 138–41; Pinnock, *Most Moved Mover*, 144–51; John Sanders, *The God Who Risks: A Theology of Divine* (Downers Grove, Ill.: IVP Academic, 2009),161, 190, 322 n. 113; John Cobb and Clark H. Pinnock, eds., *Searching for an Adequate God: A Dialogue Between Process and Free Will Theists* (Grand Rapids: William B. Eerdmans Publishing Company, 2000), 10–24, 89–90, 116–25, 166, 177–79, 183–88, 216–18; William Hasker, *Providence, Evil and the Openness of God* (London: Routledge, 2004), 137–48.

7. For a critique of Mormon views on creation, see Paul Copan and William Lane Craig, "An Examination of the Mormon Doctrine of Creation and a Defense of Creation ex nihilo," in *The New Mormon Challenge: Responding to the Latest Defenses of a Fast-Growing Movement*, ed. Francis Beckwith, Carl Mosser, and Paul Owen (Grand Rapids: Zondervan, 2002), 95–152; see also Blake Ostler's response, "Out

Open theists defend creation *ex nihilo* on both biblical and rational grounds.[8] Their position is that creation *ex nihilo* is *the* biblical doctrine of creation and that denial of the doctrine compromises God's freedom, grace, and sovereignty.[9] Our task in this paper is to show that creation *ex nihilo* is neither biblically founded nor philosophically or theologically required.

THE BIBLICAL CASE FOR CREATION EX NIHILO

Open theists often defend creation *ex nihilo* with biblical exegesis. Clark Pinnock, William Hasker, and John Sanders cite Hebrews 11:3 and Romans 4:17 as supporting their position. Hasker includes John 1:1–3 and Colossians 1:16. Sanders adds 2 Maccabees 7:28 for good measure even though most Protestants reject its canonicity.[10]

Surprisingly, not one open theist cites Genesis 1, *the* biblical creation story, as evidence of creation *ex nihilo*. Indeed, Sanders, Pinnock and Hasker admit that Genesis 1 does not support creation *ex nihilo*. Hasker's approach mirrors that of process thinkers Krensky or Griffin; he claims that Genesis 1 presupposes "the existence of a primeval chaos". Pinnock elaborates on Hasker's stance: the acts of creation as recorded in Genesis chapter 1 brought chaos under control and reintroduced God's order, but they did not eliminate the threat of this mysterious 'formless void' factor. It is a situation where, although God has the upper hand, he is not now totally in control. Scripture presents God as engaged in conflict with the powers of darkness.[11]

---

of Nothing: The History of Creation ex nihilo in Early Christian Thought," *FARMS Review of Books* 17, no. 2 (2005): 253–320. For other Mormon discussions on *creation ex nihilo,* see Keith Norman, "Ex Nihilo: The Development of the Doctrines of God and Creation in Early Christianity," *BYU Studies* 17, no. 3 (1977): 291–318. For a recent critique of creation ex nihilo from a process perspective, see David Ray Griffin, *Two Great Truths: A New Synthesis of Scientific Naturalism and Christian Faith* (Louisville: Westminster John Knox Press, 2004), especially chapter 2.

8. While we recognize that not all open theists accept creation ex nihilo, we will use the term "open theist" in this paper to represent what the group accepts on the whole.

9. See Pinnock, *Most Moved Mover,* 146; Sanders, *The God Who Risks,* 41; Cobb and Pinnock, *Searching or an Adequate God,* 21–22, 190, 220–22, 226 n. 22, 247–48. A notable exception to this general rule is Thomas Jay Oord, who considers himself to be an open theist. Oord argues against the doctrine of *creation ex nihilo* on both biblical and scientific grounds in *Defining Love: A Philosophical, Scientific, and Theological Engagement* (Ada, Mich.: Brazos Press, 2010).

10. Pinnock, *Most Moved Mover,* 146; William Hasker, "An Adequate God," in Cobb and Pinnock, *Searching for an Adequate God,* 226 note 22; Sanders, *The God Who Risks,* 41.

11. Sanders, *The God Who Risks,* 41; Hasker, "An Adequate God," 226 n. 22; Pinnock, *Most Moved Mover,* 36.

Nonetheless, Pinnock refuses to conclude that the depiction of chaos in Genesis 1 is inconsistent with creation *ex nihilo*. Instead, he claims that the "formless void" was the product of evil actions performed by fallen angels. These fallen angels were created by God *ex nihilo*, supposedly sometime before the "In the beginning" of Genesis 1:1.[12]

Citing biblical scholarship, we aim to critique open theists' argument that creation *ex nihilo* is founded in the Bible. We will examine John 1:1–3, Colossians 1:16, Hebrews 11:3, Romans 4:17, 2 Maccabees 7:28, and Wisdom of Solomon 11:17, and demonstrate how these scriptures not only fail to prove that creation *ex nihilo* is the only possible biblical interpretation, but also are more plausibly read as favoring creation *ex materia*.

In the New Jerusalem Bible, John 1:3 reads that through the Word "all things came into being, not one thing came into being except through him." James Hubler contends that "creation by word [does not] imply *ex nihilo*. . . the word [of God] functions to organize pre-cosmic matter."[13] Richard J. Clifford reminds us that John, in his prologue, draws a parallel between creation and the Christian message. Just as "darkness and chaos were overcome so that the human community can be formed, . . . the darkness and disorder resulting from unbelief are overcome by God's word and light in Christ." The parallel would fail, however, were there no chaos before creation.[14]

Hubler provides a more direct translation of John 1:3: "All things came about through him and without him not one thing came about, which came about." Recognizing an ambiguity in the verse, Hubler shares how

> the punctuation of [John 1:3] becomes critical to its meaning. Proponents of *creation ex materia* could easily qualify the creatures of the Word to that "which came about," excluding matter. Proponents of creation *ex nihilo* could place a period after "not one thing came about" and leave "which came about" to the

---

12. Pinnock, *Most Moved Mover*, 36; 146. Note that we are not here denying a "middle realm" between the divine and the human. We firmly believe in such a realm and in the reality that beings from it—both good and evil—affect this world. We simply find it implausible to say that the Genesis 1 account is best read as containing unmentioned angels—created ex nihilo by God—who are responsible for the "formless void" factor explicitly mentioned in the text.

13. James N. Hubler, "Creatio ex Nihilo: Matter, Creation, and the Body in Classical and Christian Philosophy through Aquinas" (Ph.D. diss., University of Pennsylvania, 1995), 107–8. Hubler provides the following translation of 2 Peter 3:5: "For they willingly forget that the heavens existed of old and the earth was formed from waters and by waters through the word of God." He comments that 2 Peter shows continuity with Near Eastern traditions of creation from waters. Regarding these traditions, see Hubler's chapters 1 and 3.

14. Richard J. Clifford, *Creation Accounts in the Ancient Near East and in the Bible* (Washington D.C. : Catholic Biblical Quarterly, 1994), 19.

next sentence. The absence of a determinate tradition of punctuation in New Testament texts leaves room for both interpretations.[15]

Thus, John 1:1–3 cannot support the unequivocal claim that creation *ex nihilo* is *the* biblical doctrine of creation.

Colossians 1:16 reads: "For in him were created all things in heaven and on earth: everything visible and everything invisible, thrones, ruling forces, sovereignties, powers—all things were created through him and for him" (NJB). While this verse has been cited by defenders of creation *ex nihilo*, "for proponents of creation *ex materia* the creation of all things visible and invisible is limited to what immediately precedes and follows in the verse: 'all things in the heavens and upon earth.' The invisible are the angelic powers: the thrones, [ruling forces], [sovereignties], powers."[16] By understanding "all things" to mean the existence of the many beings existing in heaven and earth, a reader need not think that Paul is affirming that matter itself was created.

Like John 1:3, Colossians 1:16 does not describe *how* God created the world; rather, it emphasizes Christ's lordship over creation. In view of the Colossians' apparent indulgence in angel worship (2:18), Paul directs their attention to Christ. According to Gerhard May, "Until the beginning of the second century there was for Christian thought no alternative to the elementary confession that God created heaven and earth." Those who read creation *ex nihilo* into Colossians 1:16 (and John 1:3) "consider statements in the text from the standpoint of questions which did not yet exist in this form for Paul and John." Given these considerations, Colossians 1:16 does not positively espouse creation *ex nihilo*, but is found when one comes with an *ex nihilo* theological background.[17]

Hebrews 11:3 also refers to the visible and invisible: "It is by faith that we understand that the ages were created by a word from God, so that from the invisible the visible world came to be" (NJB).[18] Paul's words suggest creation *ex nihilo* only when we assume that "the invisible" refers to absolute nothingness. Philip E. Hughes points out, "It is not the custom of Scripture to equate invisibility with non-existence; quite the contrary in fact, for, as Paul says, it is precisely the things which are not seen that are eternal (something that cannot be said of a nonentity!) and the things which are seen that are

---

15. Hubler, "Creatio ex Nihilo," 108.

16. Ibid, 109.

17. Paul Beasley-Murray, "Colossians," *Pauline Studies: Essays Presented to Professor F. F. Bruce on his 70ᵗʰ Birthday*, ed. Donald H. Agner and Murray J. Harris (Grand Rapids: Eerdmans, 1980), 172–73. Gerhard May, *Creation Ex Nihilo: The Doctrine of Creation out of Nothing in Early Christian Thought* (London: Bloomsbury T&T Clark, 2004), 26 note 104.

18. The KJV translates this word—*aiōens* (literally "ages")—as "worlds."

impermanent."[19] Commentators who use the Bible to prove creation *ex nihilo* read into the text their own theological biases.

Romans 4:17 also fails to establish creation *ex nihilo*. It reads, "God . . . quickeneth the dead, and calleth those things which be not as though they were" (KJV). A translator who assumes creation *ex nihilo* might understand this last clause as C. E. B. Cranfield did—God "calls things which are not into being."[20] However, James Hubler points out that the phrase "things which are not . . . need not be understood in an absolute sense of non-being," but may instead refer "to the previous non-existence of those things which are now brought into existence. There is no direct reference to the absence or presence of a material cause."[21] Michael Lodahl suggests that God's resurrecting the dead is synonymous with calling "those things which be not as though they were."[22] His interpretation is plausible because the resurrection is mentioned in the verse.

There is also a syntactical problem with an *ex nihilo* reading of Romans 4:17: Paul uses the Greek adverb *hōs*, which generally means "as," "like as," or "according as". According to Douglas Moo, if Paul means to discuss God's

---

19. Phillip E. Hughes, *A Commentary on the Epistle to the* Hebrews (Grand Rapids: Eerdmans, 1977), 74. Hughes speculates that the "invisible" realities of which Hebrews 11:3 speaks to be the "power and energy that are, so to speak, released and organized by God's utterance of his commanding word" (Hughes, *Creatio ex Nihilo*, 76). But the Bible makes such a reading of "the invisible" highly unlikely. As Hughes points out, 2 Corinthians 4:18 refers to things invisible to us that are nonetheless eternal. Furthermore, claiming that God creates invisible things entails creation out of non-existence is problematic because scripture also attests of God's invisibility, which surely cannot mean God's non-existence. See 1 Tim. 1:17 and Heb. 11:27.2

20. C.E.B. Cranfield, *Romans: A Shorter Commentary* (Grand Rapids: Eerdmans, 1985), 93.

21. James Hubler, *Creatio ex Nihilo*, 109.

22. Michael Lodahl, "Creation Out of Nothing? Or is Next to Nothing Enough?" *Thy Nature and Thy Name is Love: Wesleyan and Process Theologies in Dialogue*, ed. Bryan P. Stone and Thomas Jay Oord (Nashville: Kingswood Books, 2001). Lodahl states: "If the Hebrew Bible is, at best, ambiguous on the issue of *ex nihilo*, the Christian Testament's testimony is equally indistinct even if one argues that the evidence is implicitly present. A traditionally favored text is Romans 4:17 where Paul describes God as the One 'who gives life to the dead and calls into existence the things that do not exist.' This is obviously a creation passage, but it is not particularly obvious that the creative activity described is *ex nihilo*. In fact, since Paul is offering Jesus' resurrection from the dead as the decisive exemplification of God's creative activity, a creation from nothing is precisely *not* what is suggested. God does not 'create' the resurrected Christ *ex nihilo*, for the resurrection is indeed the glorious . . . reanimating of the crucified Jesus who indeed bears his wounds even in the resurrection state" (220).

creative activity, "it is surprising that he speaks of God's calling things 'as though' they existed; we would have expected him to say 'calls things into being'." Moo concludes "somewhat hesitantly and reluctantly, that the clause cannot refer to God's creative power as such, whether general or spiritual."[23] John Murray and Grant Osborne agree that the verse does not refer to creation. So do Luther and Pelagius, who favored creation *ex nihilo*. Since the subject of Romans 4 is the faith of Abraham, which secured for him a great posterity, the things "which be not as though they were" may refer to Abraham's future children, not all of creation.[24]

Sanders claims 2 Maccabees 7:28 suggests creation *ex nihilo*. It reads, "I beg you, child, to look at the heavens and the earth and see all that is in them; then you will know that God did not make them out of existing things; and in the same way the human race came into existence" (NAB). At first glance, you couldn't ask for a more straightforward scriptural affirmation of creation *ex nihilo* than "God did not make [the heavens and the earth] out of existing things." However, significant scholarship tells us our first impression is a false one. For Gerhard May, the verse "implies no more than the conception that the world came into existence through the sovereign creative act of God, and that it previously was not there."[25] James Hubler concurs, arguing that the idea of "non-being" in 2 Maccabees 7:28 "refers to the non-existence of the heavens and earth before God's creative act. It does not express absolute non-existence, only the prior non-existence of heaven and earth."[26] Frances Young argues that in 2 Maccabees 7:28 "there is no 'theory' of creation out of nothing. . . . [For Jews,] God could conceivably bring into existence 'things' which do not exist before, without such language excluding a pre-existent 'stuff'."[27] David Winston believes the verse refers to "unformed primordial matter." According to Maren Niehoff, "This famous statement, which has often been taken as evidence for an early Jewish notion of creation *ex nihilo*,

23. Joseph Thayer, *Thayer's Greek-English Lexicon of the New Testament: Coded with Strong's Concordance Numbers* (Peabody, Mass.: Hendrickson Publishers, 1995), 680. Douglas J. Moo, *The Epistle to the Romans* (Grand Rapids: Eerdmans, 1996), 282, 287.

24. John Murray, *Epistle to the Romans* (Grand Rapids: Eerdmans, 1997), 146. Grant Osborne, *Romans* (Downers Grove, Ill., 2010), 117.

25. May, *Creatio ex Nihilo*, 7.

26. Hubler, *Creatio ex Nihilo*, 90.

27. Francis Young, "Creatio Ex Nihilo: A Context for the Emergence of Christian Doctrine of Creation," *Scottish Journal of Theology* 44 (1991): 144. Young, a strong proponent of the doctrine's Christological and soteriological import, declares that ex nihilo creation is not a Jewish idea but rather a Christian doctrine made after the New Testament materials were composed (141–44).

rather seems to convey Platonic ontology, suggesting that [unformed] matter does not belong to the realm of real existence."[28]

2 Maccabees 7:28 should be examined in its historical context. Jonathan Goldstein estimates the source for this verse was written during the period between 159 and 132 BCE.[29] The earliest evidence of creation *ex nihilo* among the Jews is not found until sometime in the first few decades after the destruction of the Temple in 70 CE.[30] Winston claims there is prima facie evidence that creation *ex nihilo* was not accepted by rabbis during this period.[31]

Open theists, who depend on the Bible to explain why they support creation *ex nihilo*, will find little to no biblical support. Peter Hayman has said "nearly all recent studies on the origin of the doctrine of creation *ex nihilo* have come to the conclusion that this doctrine is not native to Judaism, is nowhere attested in the Hebrew Bible, and probably arose in Christianity in the second century C.E. in the course of its fierce battle with Gnosticism."[32] Michael DeRoche has said the same in other words: "Although the Hebrew Bible contains a variety of cosmogonic traditions, most agree that God creates the universe by imposing order on a primeval, pre-created chaos."[33] In Isaiah

28. Maren R. Niehoff, "Creatio ex Nihilo Theology in Genesis Rabbah in Light of Christian Exegesis," *Harvard Theological Review* 99 (2005): 44.

29. Jonathan Goldstein, *II Maccabees*, 48.

30. Goldstein states "that the patriarch Rabban Gamaliel II asserted [*creation ex nihilo*] unambiguously, within a few decades after the destruction of the Temple in 70 C.E." Jonathan A. Goldstein, "The Origins of the Doctrine of Creation Ex Nihilo," *Journal of Jewish Studies* 35, no. 2 (1984): 187. Niehoff, however, finds evidence that the story in which Rabban Gamaliel II is portrayed as teaching *creation ex nihilo* is "pseudepigraphic, attributing statements to Gamaliel which he himself never made" (Niehoff, *Creatio ex Nihilo Theology*, 49). He argues that the entrance of *creation ex nihilo* into Judaism was a third or fourth century adoption from post–New Testament Christianity.

31. David Winston, "The book of Wisdom's Theory of Cosmogony," *History of Religions* 11, no. 2 (1971): 191. Ten examples are given in *Mekilta, Shirta* 8 to describe the uniqueness of God's acts in contrast to those of man, but the best example of all, that God can make things out of nothing, is not given. Moreover, example six states that to make a roof man requires wood, stones, dirt, and water, whereas God has made a roof for his world out of water. God's first act of creation thus presupposes the existence of water."

32. Peter Hayman, "Monotheism—A Misused Word in Jewish Studies?" *Journal of Jewish Studies* 42 (1991): 3. For more on the history of the doctrine, see Edwin Hatch, *The Influence of Greek Ideas on Christianity* (New York: Harper Torchbook, 1957). See also Keith Norman, "Ex Nihilo."

33. Michael DeRoche, "Isaiah XLV 7 and the Creation of Chaos?" *Vetus Testamentum* 42, no. 1 (January 1992): 11. We should not understand DeRoche's phrase "pre-created" as implying God first created chaotic matter and subsequently

2 and Job, Psalms, and Proverbs we find language illustrating Yahweh's containment of primordial oceans that continually threaten the ordered world In the New Testament, "[Christ's] resurrection is interpreted as a new creation because Christ, the representative human being, has defeated death, the enemy of the race and hence of the world. Christ's act is like the defeat of darkness and the waters (the primordial human enemy) in the first creation."[34]

If we extend the canon to the Apocrypha (as Sanders does, appealing to 2 Maccabees 7:28), opponents of creation *ex nihilo* have an ally in the Wisdom of Solomon. To illustrate God's omnipotence, the author speaks of God's "all-powerful hand, which has created the world out of formless matter" (Wisdom of Solomon 11:17). Responding to those who nonetheless affirm an ancient Jewish belief in creation *ex nihilo*, David Winston states that the "first explicit formulation of creation *ex nihilo* appeared in second-century Christian literature, where the argument for a 'double creation' theory is made on the grounds that creation out of an eternal primordial element would compromise the sovereignty of God." After reviewing the relevant historical and contextual evidence, Winston concludes, "there is no reason to doubt the plain meaning of [the author's] statement [Wisdom of Solomon 11:17] that creation was out of formless matter." Given the weight of exegetical evidence against it, open theists should be wary to affirm creation *ex nihilo* as *the* biblical doctrine of creation.[35]

Open theists should not forget their commitment to scriptural texts. While Gregory Boyd does not share this view, he indicates that those who "believe in the infallible authority of Scripture" a "comprehensive investigation of God's word" is how difficulties are settled.[36] Pinnock declares that adherence to a

---

created everything else from that created matter (a two-stage creation similar to the one Copan and Craig propose in *Creation out of Nothing*). Later in the article, DeRoche argues that "Isa. xlv 7 is thought to be the sole exception to the notion that chaos is pre-created and independent of the deity" (12), and then argues that Isaiah 45:7 does not in fact teach that God created chaos. By "pre-created," DeRoche seems to have in mind something existing before the creation of the world, something ontologically independent of God's creative activity.

34. Clifford, "Creation in the Psalms," *Creation in the Biblical Traditions*, ed. Richard J. Clifford and John J. Collins (Washington D.C.: The Catholic Biblical Quarterly, 1992), 61–69. See also, Gale A. Yee, "The Theology of Creation in Proverbs 8," in *Creation in the Biblical Traditions*, ed. Richard J. Clifford and John J. Collins (Washington D.C.: The Catholic Biblical Quarterly, 1992), 87–96. Clifford, "The Bible," 19.

35. David Winston, *The Wisdom of Solomon: A New Translation with Introduction and Commentary* (NY: Doubleday, 1979), 191–92.

36. Gregory A. Boyd, *God of the Possible: A Biblical Introduction to the Open View of God* (Grand Rapids: Baker Books, 2000), 24. Pinnock, *Most Moved Mover*, 24.

theological position requires "biblical backing and resonance."[37] Defending creation *ex nihilo* on biblical grounds fails to fulfill this commitment.[38]

THE RATIONAL CASE FOR CREATION *EX NIHILO*

Open theists suggest reason is an acceptable route to theological truth.[39] In *The Openness of God*, Pinnock et al. leave their arguments "open to question," and "welcome the discussion [they] hope [their arguments] will generate."[40] We accept their invitation and echo their hope of generating further discussion on this issue.

In the following sections, we examine and critique the following arguments open theists have given in support of creation *ex nihilo*: (1) the openness/social Trinity model solves the problems surrounding God's perfect love prior to a creation *ex nihilo*; (2) God satisfied no need of his own in the creation; and (3) only a God who creates *ex nihilo* is adequately free, gracious, and sovereign.

THE LOVE IN SOCIAL TRINITY
DOES NOT NECESSITATE CREATION

One criticism of creation *ex nihilo* raised by process theologians is that if God cannot be perfectly loving without an object of love outside himself, and if no part of the actualized universe existed prior to God's creative act, then God created from necessity; however, if God created from necessity, then God had no choice in the matter, and this contradicts the openness claim that God's creative act was performed out of freedom, grace, and sovereignty.

Open theists believe that their social model of the Trinity avoids this difficulty. "The triune God, unlike the God in process theism," writes Pinnock, "does not need the world to make up for a love and mutuality lacking in his

---

37. Pinnock, *Most Moved Mover*, 19.

38. Boyd, *God of the Possible*, 24; Pinnock, *Most Moved Mover*, 19.

39. Although open theists believe the Bible, tradition, reason, and experience are all important factors in forming a theological method, "agreement with Scripture is the most important test for any theological proposal. By definition, the task of Christian theology is to interpret the contents of the Bible" (Rice, "Biblical," 16). We admit many have found support for creation *ex nihilo* in the Bible. But one can also find support for exhaustive, specific foreknowledge, predestination, salvation for only the elect, and so forth, which is exactly why Richard Rice writes, "The crucial question is whether the idea is faithful to the overall biblical portrait of God—the picture that emerges from the full range of biblical evidence" (Rice, "Biblical," 15). It is our contention that the idea of creation *ex nihilo* is not faithful to the full range of biblical evidence.

40. "Preface" to Pinnock, *Openness of God*, 10.

nature." God is "internally social and self-sufficient". Therefore, "God did not need to create." Specifically, "God did not need to create in order to love, for the Trinity experiences and manifests a fullness of love." Because God did not need to create, "the creation is a free and gracious decision on God's part."[41]

The foregoing seems like an adequate answer to the above "need-for-love" argument posed by the process theists; however, one wonders how open theists consistently maintain a strict notion of monotheism if, by their own Trinitarian model, the divine persons must be sufficiently distinct from one another to fulfill the need for *other*-love. We invite open theists to consider the following questions: If love of others is required for the divine nature, before creation, were the members of the trinity sufficiently different, so that their need to love others did not necessitate creation? For instance, the Trinitarian community may have not been sufficiently other if the members always existed in this relationship without choosing it, or if the members were not significantly different from one another or had no needs or desires that the others could fulfill. In other words, is the love of God in the Trinity even meaningful, for how can love be expressed among beings who have no need but the need to love, and cannot hurt or help each other in any way? Without showing how the love within the Trinity is sufficiently a love of others, the Open Theists may be vulnerable to the Process Theist critique.

THE SOCIAL TRINITY AS SELF-SUFFICIENT

Open theists generally claim that because God's life was complete before creation, God did not create the world out of any need. Pinnock offers the following analogy:

> Imagine a happily married couple, already fulfilled in their love for one another, having a baby. Having a baby is something they could freely choose to do and they would certainly love it. But one must say that, while their love for the child expresses their love for one another, they are not required to have the child, they are not required to have a child in order to love. God's love for the world expresses his loving essence too, but it is not a necessary expression of his essence. . . . To put it bluntly, *God's nature would be complete and his love fulfilled even without a world to love.*[42]

Hasker agrees with Pinnock's conclusion. He asserts that the life of God

---

41. Clark H. Pinnock, "Systematic Theology," *The Openness of God: A Biblical Challenge to the Traditional Understanding of God*, ed. Clark Pinnock, et al. (Downers Grove, Ill.: InterVarsity, 1994), 108–9; Sanders, *The God Who Risks*, 41, 176; Hasker, "In Response," in *Searching or an Adequate God: A Dialogue Between Process and Free Will Theists*, ed. John Cobb and Clark H. Pinnock (Grand Rapids: William B. Eerdmans Publishing Company, 2000), 47.

42. Pinnock, *Most Moved Mover*, 145; emphasis added.

is completely rich, fulfilling and satisfying without reference to creation, and therefore. . . . God has no need whatever for a created world in order for the divine life to be complete and perfect. Insofar as it makes sense to quantify such matters, we may say that God's life is infinitely satisfying, and the satisfaction cannot be increased by anything that might be added by a created order.[43]

Sanders offers an alternative approach, claiming that God *chooses* to be in need: "Although God does not need the world in order to experience love, God is free to create beings with whom to share his love and with whom he shares their love. . . . Thus in this restricted sense it can be said that God has chosen to be in 'need'."[44]

However, Pinnock and Hasker's assertion that God satisfies no need or desire through creation may not be coherent. LDS philosopher Blake Ostler provides the following argument to show that incoherence follows if one accepts the criterion of sufficient reason:

1. If God exists and possesses aseity, then he is not dependent on anything nor lacking in any conceivable manner (i.e., God is self-sufficient).
2. A self-sufficient being cannot manifest a need nor be enhanced by any positive action (1).
3. Every positive action requires an explanation sufficient to account for it (Criteri[on] of Sufficient Reason).
4. Creation of the cosmos is a positive action.
5. A self-sufficient being could not manifest a reason sufficient to explain why it preferred existence of the cosmos to its nonexistence (1, 2).
6. Hence, God did not create the cosmos (3, 4, 5).[45]

This argument hinges on (3), which appears intuitively plausible. When the criterion of sufficient reason is conjoined with the absoluteness of God, the result is a *reductio ad absurdum*—God did not create. Or perhaps one might assert God creates fortuitously, but such seems hardly consistent with the divine nature. To avoid these conclusions Open Theists must reject the criterion, but what basis do Open Theists have for doing so?

For Mormons, God's commitment to help co-existent intelligences necessitates creation. In fact, God could not experience equal joy with and without creation. In the words of the late scientist and Mormon apostle John Widstoe:

> The progress of intelligent beings is a mutual affair. A lone God in the universe cannot find great joy in his power. . . . The development of intelligence increases the variety within the universe, for each active individual may bring new relation-

---

43. Hasker, *Providence, Evil and the Openness of God*, 182.
44. Sanders, *The God Who Risk*, 185.
45. Blake Ostler, *Exploring Mormon Thought: The Attributes of God* (Salt Lake City: Greg Kofford Books, 2001), 90.

ships into view, and thus increase manifold the body of acquired truth. In that sense, the man who progresses through his increase in knowledge and power becomes a co-laborer with God, and may be said, indeed, to be a help to God. It is a comforting thought, that not only do we need God but that God also needs us.[46]

CREATION *EX NIHILO* AND THE FREEDOM, GRACE, AND SOVEREIGNTY OF GOD

Open theists find both process and Mormon views on creation unacceptable, primarily because they believe that both result in a less-than-adequate conception of God. Pinnock writes, "The problem in process theology seems to be the fact that it requires us to view the world as necessary to God, with the implication that God is not free in creation but necessarily tied to a world."[47] In open theism, God's perfect self-sufficiency renders God's creating a free and gracious act. Additionally, God is absolutely sovereign in open theism; all things are contingent on God for their existence. Although Pinnock prefers to focus on God's love for creatures, he is "impressed" by God's power to create *ex nihilo*.[48] Perhaps open theists are influenced by the "majesty" of the doctrine, especially when it is contrasted to its "less impressive" alternative. For example, after quoting several passages in Job that powerfully portray God's sovereignty in relation to creation, Hasker asks, "Isn't the majesty of God as creator seen here as an integral aspect of the very Godhood of God? Could we reduce the creative role of God to that prescribed by Whitehead without undermining the entire conception of God that is being presented?"[49]

---

46. John Widtsoe, *Rational Theology as Taught by the Church of Jesus Christ of Latter-day Saints* (Salt Lake City: Deseret News, 1915), 27–28.

47. Pinnock, "Systematic Theology," 108–9.

48. Pinnock, *The Openness of God*. It surely would be impressive for a being to create the universe out of nothing, as if by sheer command. However, while we would certainly admire such ability, the idea of a being creating the universe—in the sense of organizing it out of chaos—is impressive in a different way. On either model, the end result is the same: the universe we see around us, whether created out of chaos or created out of nothing, is what it is. All else being equal, if X could bring, say, the Taj Mahal into existence out of nothing, and Y could bring about the exact same structure using already existing or uncreated materials, who would accomplish the more impressive feat, X or Y? The two buildings would be replicas of each other. Thus, we couldn't examine them in order to ascertain the answer to the question. If we argue that X is more impressive than Y because X did it by mere fiat, then all we've done is form a subjective value judgment, admiring power itself, regardless of the good ends it accomplishes.

49. Hasker, "An Adequate," 221.

Michael Lodahl explains in detail why creation *ex nihilo* is so theologically attractive. Open theists should agree with the following:

> If there is some element or aspect of our universe that exists not because God calls it into being but *just because*, then there is something of which God is not truly God. This idea is theologically repugnant, at least from a traditional perspective, because it implies a dualism of 'God and something else' and thus severely compromises the divine uniqueness and sovereignty; similarly, it is religiously repugnant because it means that our worship of God is directed toward a power that is less than ultimate.[50]

One wonders whether open theists are guilty of speculating from *dignum deo* ("that which it is dignified for God to be"). While it may be appropriate to practice theology on the basis of norms, doing so has led to many contra-biblical ideas about God, such as impassibility, which open theists have shown to stand in sharp contrast to biblical revelation. Pinnock has observed the consequence of *dignum deo* reasoning:

> What we [Christians] are doing, in effect, is seeking to correct the Bible; to derive truth about God . . . from our own intuitions of what is "fitting" for God to be. In this way God's nature is made to conform to our notions of what deity should be like and, if the Bible does not measure up to this standard in its speech about God, we invoke our own subjective criteria to correct it.[51]

Pinnock also admits that *ex nihilo* creation has led to the acceptance of many unbiblical divine attributes.[52] If so, creation ex nihilo may be in tension with the open theist project to recover the God portrayed in the Bible.

CREATION *EX MATERIA* AND THE FREEDOM OF GOD

Having surveyed the openness arguments for creation ex nihilo, we now examine the philosophical case for a God that creates *ex materia*. First, creation from pre-existing materials does not suggest God was compelled to organize them. God is free to create as he pleases. If these pre-existing materials are necessarily co-eternal with God and God must necessarily create from them if he is to create at all, as Process and Mormon theologies accept, then there are uncreated restraints on God's power. Such constraints entail that God did not have complete liberty in choosing to create a world amongst all logical possibilities, in order for it to possess the least amount of moral and natural evils. Thus, openness theologians are correct in claiming God's creation is not free in this sense. That God creates is up to him, but what he creates is constrained by a set of not logical possibilities, but by a set of pos-

---

50. Lodahl, "Creation out of Nothing?" 221.
51. Pinnock, *Most Moved Moveer,* 67.
52. Ibid., 77–79.

sibilities determined by the inherent capacity of the mass-energy with which he works. Yet neither Mormons nor process thinkers see this as objectionable. This thesis largely absolves God from being ultimately responsible for many of the horrible outcomes of power that are witnessed in this world, as some power is essentially beyond God's full control.

CREATION *EX MATERIA* AND THE GRACE OF GOD

For open theism, the needlessness of creation confirms God's graciousness and benevolence. [53] "In grace," Sanders argues, "God created and embarked on this program[,] and in grace God invites us to participate as significant partners with him."[54]

Mormons also believe God's creative act was gracious, even though he created by restructuring pre-existing materials. It at least makes sense to say God could be gracious and benevolent towards co-existent beings. On the other hand, it is unclear whether God can be gracious to that which is not. Was he not gracious towards what is logically possible to exist, but in fact does not (the centaur, Pegasus and the mermaid)?

Another problem for the open theist belief in a gracious creation is that some of God's creations do not agree with God's ultimate purposes and will end up in hell. Sanders has made clear that,

> The doctrine of hell . . . implies the failure of humans to reciprocate the divine love and the failure of God to reclaim everyone. If some people ultimately refuse to love God and God will not force their love, then what else is God to do? Unless one affirms either universalism or double predestination, it must be concluded that God's project ends in failure for some.[55]

While one may argue that existence in hell is preferable to non-existence (and it may not be), admitting of hell at least lessens the graciousness of God's creation *ex nihilo*. The problem of hell may also arise for Mormons but it is mitigated by the doctrine of pre-existence, and by a unique definition of hell and by an expansive and unfixed eschatology.

In Mormon theology, everyone who lives or has lived on the earth understood the general risk entailed in coming to earth but chose to come nonetheless, rejoicing in the opportunity it presented for divine progression.[56] Thus,

---

53. Richard Rice, "Process Theism and the Open View of God: The Crucial Difference," in *Searching or an Adequate God: A Dialogue Between Process and Free Will Theists*, ed. John Cobb and Clark H. Pinnock (Grand Rapids: William B. Eerdmans Publishing Company, 2000), 185.

54. Sanders, *The God Who Risks*, 169.

55. Ibid., 230.

56. Mormons often quote Job 38:7 in reference to this idea. David Paulsen and Blake Ostler, "Sin, Suffering, and Soul-Making," *Revelation, Reason and Faith*, ed.

all those consigned to "eternal punishment" for having usurped their agency against God recognized the consequences of participation in God's plan. The responsibility for their failure can ultimately be traced to them, rather than to God—as might be the case had he created them *ex nihilo*.

In addition, even those consigned to "eternal punishment" still have the possibility of redemption. A revelation recorded by Joseph Smith teaches: "It is not written that there shall be no end to this [punishment], but it is written *endless [punishment]*. For, behold, I am endless, and the punishment which is given from my hand is endless punishment. . . . Wherefore—Eternal punishment is God's punishment"; but "the end thereof, neither the place thereof, nor their torment, no man knows" (D&C 19:6,10–12; 76:45). Accordingly, even *eternal* or *endless* hell may have an end, and every person will receive the opportunity and option to accept Christ's gospel (D&C 138) and to enjoy existence at some level of heaven (D&C 76).[57] A person can dwell in a kingdom of glory if she chooses to abide by its laws (D&C 88).

Besides Mormons, process theists like David Ray Griffin conceive of redemption and soul-building continuing in the eschaton. Instead of sending us to hell, Griffin believes that in time God will love the hell out of us.[58] The eschaton is thus less a problem to reconcile with a gracious creation for Mormon and process thinkers than for openness thinkers.

CREATION *EX MATERIA* AND THE SOVEREIGNTY OF GOD

Open theologians criticize the process God for his inability to unilaterally accomplish his purposes or to promise a successful outcome for creation. He can only invite, persuade, and entice, making creaturely response essential to God's victory. "However, unlike proponents of process theism," openness thinkers "maintain that God does retain the right to intervene unilaterally in earthly affairs."[59] In this way, the openness view holds onto "the biblical hope in a definitive victory over evil at the end."[60]

This is perhaps a point where Mormons feel closer to open theists than to process theists. Mormon theology defends creation *ex materia* while eschewing

Donald W. Parry, et al. (Provo: Foundation for Ancient Research and Mormon Studies, 2002), 260–61.

57. Mormons believe in celestial, terrestrial, and telestial heavens, each varying in glory and opportunity. God is said to dwell in the celestial kingdom.

58. Griffin, *Two Great Truths,* 113.

59. David Basinger, "Practical Implications," in *The Openness of God: A Biblical Challenge to the Traditional Understanding of God,* ed. Clark Pinnock, et al. (Downers Grove, Ill.: InterVarsity, 1994), 159.

60. Pinnock, *Most Moved Mover,* 144.

the process model of divine power. God *prefers* persuasion to coercion, and may be morally obligated to use constraint and apply persuasive power on the whole, but we also believe that God is a powerful agent who can and does intervene in history to fulfill his purposes and promises.[61] Christ's victory over sin and death is a prime example of God's active, personal involvement. Moreover, Mormons believe the biblical affirmation that Christ will eventually return to establish peace.[62] Thus, Mormons reject *ex nihilo* creation while still retaining a strong, albeit a non-absolutist understanding of God's sovereignty.

While creation *ex nihilo* certainly "implies that God has the power to intervene in the world," creation *ex materia* does not imply the opposite.[63] Jonathan Goldstein reasons that belief in divine omnipotence would not have required Jews or Christians of the early Christian era to affirm creation *ex nihilo*: "[Many] found it possible to believe in a god who was omnipotent even though he created the universe from pre-existent matter. It was no detraction from the deity's power if he could not create a logical impossibility, such as a square circle, and for many thinkers creation *ex nihilo* was just such an impossibility."[64]

Jon D. Levenson agrees:

> The absolute sovereignty of the God of Israel is not a simple given in the Hebrew Bible. . . . Instead, YHWH's mastery is often fragile, in continual need of reac-

61. Taken in conjunction with creation *ex nihilo*, Griffin finds this idea rationally repugnant and morally demotivating ("Process Theology and the Christian," 14–24), but we, like open theists, take comfort that God can save the world from ultimate destruction. We believe that God generally does not intervene to prevent evil. To do so would trample on freedom—something Mormons believe is inherent in each human—and frustrate one of the essential purposes of mortal existence—to develop into godly persons, a process that could not take place in an environment void of opposition and pain. In Mormon theology, the doctrine of the atonement promises that our losses will be made up to us in the resurrection if we prove faithful. For an openness/process discussion of these issues, see Hasker and Griffin's dialogue in *Process Studies* 29, no. 2 (2000): 194–236.

62. See, for example, Revelations 21:1–4. However, according to Mormon theology, creation is eternally ongoing. Thus, the eschatological vision of John does not mean that death and pain will end in an ultimate and final sense.

63. Pinnock, "Systematic Theology," 109.

64. Goldstein, 188. David Winston similarly states that "For Jewish mystics, creation out of nothing (i.e., out of absolute nothing) belonged to the realm of the logically absurd." He quotes the following from Rabbi Ezra ben Shelomo's *Commentary on the Song of Songs*: "[God's] inability to create something out of nothing does not indicate any deficiency on his part, even as it does not indicate any deficiency on his part that He is unable to produce what is logically absurd." Winston, "The Book of Wisdom's," 198.

tivation and reassertion, and at times, as in the laments, painfully distant from ordinary experience, a memory and a hope rather than a current reality. It is, in short, a confession of faith. . . . What makes this [a] confession of faith . . . rather than a shallow truism is the survival of those potent forces of chaos that were subjugated and domesticated at creation.[65]

Levenson contends that the concern of creation theology in the Hebrew Bible is not creation *ex nihilo* but creation *ex chaos*—a chaos still prevalent and recalcitrant in the world, a chaos over which God himself has promised to ultimately prevail. The premise that only an *ex nihilo* creator can be sovereign is not found in the Hebrew Bible.[66] We agree that God's ultimate victory is contingent on a promise, not on a philosophical proof. We trust God because of our faith, not because of our philosophy. Yet if creation *ex nihilo* is simply assumed to guarantee God's success and sovereignty, one can just as freely assume God creates *ex materia* and yet possesses enough power over creation to achieve his purposes. Thus, the desire to secure God's success does not require accepting creation from nothing. However, Mormons tend to see God's sovereignty as not apodictic, but as encountered in practice, history, and in personal religious experience.

In this regard we find ourselves agreeing with Pinnock when he wrote, "It is the wisdom of God that we marvel at, not abstract omniscience. . . . Our assurance [of God's victory] is based, not on a rational system, but on God's promise and on his track record. God does not promise things he cannot deliver. He is not an insecure deity who needs to control everything and foreknow everything in order to accomplish anything!" We extend Pinnock's position when we affirm that God's promise and "track record" prove he is sufficiently both knowing and powerful to achieve ultimate victory.[67]

---

65. John D. Levenson, *Creation and the Persistence of Evil: The Jewish Drama of Divine Omnipotence* (Princeton: Princeton University Press, 1988), 47.

66. While it may be logically possible that some being could ultimately thwart God's purposes, it is ontologically impossible. That is, such a state of affairs could not be obtained in the real world. The Christian theologian Hermogenes offered a similar argument. He "emphatically declared that matter cannot be a principle of equal rank ontologically with God. God is Lord over matter, and this proposition is turned into an argument for the eternity of matter: God was in his unchangeableness always Lord, and so there must have been from eternity something for him to be Lord of. He is not comparable with any other being, the first, the sole Lord and creator of everything, and in the power of his lordship he uses matter for his creation." Hermogenes found biblical basis for this doctrine in Genesis 1. May, *Creatio ex Nihilo*, 141–42.

67. Pinnock, *Most Moved Mover*, 52.

CONCLUSION

We have attempted to demonstrate that the openness case for creation *ex nihilo* is neither biblically required nor philosophically compelling. The Bible does not plausibly support creation *ex nihilo*, but favors creation *ex materia*. Mormons deny creation *ex nihilo* without compromising the freedom, grace, and sovereignty of God. Although the terms must be understood differently, a God who brings order out of uncreated chaos can do so freely, graciously, and supremely. The idea that God would have been perfectly happy without creating may render our existence arbitrary. Contra openness thinkers, Mormons believe that God faces many difficult obstacles, which are part of the very nature of reality. Contra process thinkers, Mormons believe God can subdue every enemy and fulfill every promise. We recommend that open theists continue to rid themselves of unbiblical ideas by rejecting creation *ex nihilo*.[68]

68. Preston Campbell, Garrett Sens, Louis Midgley, Blake Ostler, Michael Pennock, Martin Pulido, Laura Rawlins, Taylor Rouanzion, Mel Thorne and Kaitlyn Tolman have critically read earlier drafts of this paper and offered helpful suggestions as to form and content. The authors gratefully acknowledge the financial support for this project provided by the College of Humanities and Department of Philosophy at BYU.

Publication of *Element* is made possible
with the assistance and expertise of
Greg Kofford Books

www.ingramcontent.com/pod-product-compliance
Lightning Source LLC
Chambersburg PA
CBHW071422040426
42445CB00012BA/1251